A Philos‹

A Philosophy of Fear

Lars Svendsen

Translated by John Irons

REAKTION BOOKS

Published by Reaktion Books Ltd
33 Great Sutton Street
London EC1V 0DX, UK

www.reaktionbooks.co.uk

First published in English 2008

This book was first published in 2007 by
Universitetsforlaget, Oslo under the title *Frykt*
by Lars Fr. H. Svendsen
Copyright © Universitetsforlaget 2007

English-language translation © Reaktion Books 2008

English translation by John Irons

This translation has been published with the financial support of NORLA

Printed and bound in Great Britain by
CPI/Antony Rowe, Chippenham, Wiltshire

British Library Cataloguing in Publication Data

Svendsen, Lars Fr. H., 1970–
A philosophy of fear
1. Fear 2. Fear – Social aspects
I. Title
152.4'6

ISBN 978 1 86189 404 5

Contents

'Why can't love ever touch my heart like fear does?'
The The, 'Bluer than Midnight', *Dusk* (1993)

Preface

This book is a result of my increasing irritation at the colonization of our life-world by fear. Books motivated by irritation have a tendency to be polemical, and this book is no exception. It is an attack on the tendency to consider practically all phenomena from a perspective of fear. A paradoxical trait of the culture of fear is that it emerges at a time when, by all accounts, we are living more securely than ever before in human history. One of my most important arguments against the culture of fear is that it undermines our freedom.

It might seem strange to be writing a book about our living in a culture of fear after having previously written a book about our living in a culture of boredom. The two diagnoses of our present culture as being one of fear and one of boredom respectively would seem on the face of it to be contradictory. If one is consumed by fear, one is not bored. But every life will contain both elements. In the poem 'Dockery and Son' (1963), Philip Larkin seems to imply that these two emotions, broadly speaking, sum up human existence: 'Life is first boredom, then fear.'

Every society – and not least postmodern ones – is characterized by many contrasting movements and phenomena. Two phenomena such as boredom and fear, however, do not simply oppose each other but can also build up under each other. Fear is not simply something we are exposed to against our will; it is often also something we voluntarily expose ourselves to in an attempt to transcend a banal, boring everyday existence. I attempt in this book to unravel what kind of an emotion fear is, what role it plays in present-day culture and, not least, what political use is made of it.

The book consists of seven chapters. In chapter One I give a brief account of 'the culture of fear', that is, how fear has become a kind of culturally determined magnifying glass through which we consider the world. Chapter Two is an attempt to describe what kind of a phenomenon fear is, and adopts a number of different approaches, ranging from neurobiology to phenomenology. In chapter Three I examine the role of fear in 'the risk society' and demonstrate how our attempts to minimize risk contain many irrational aspects. Chapter Four deals with the fact that we often voluntarily seek what is frightening – in extreme sports and entertainment, for example – something that is paradoxical, taking into consideration that we normally try to avoid sources of fear. In chapter Five I take a look at the concept of trust and point out that the culture of fear has an undermining effect on trust – something that in turn increases the scope of fear. When general trust decreases, this has a disintegrating effect on social relations, although fear for its part can also have an integrating effect. This integrating role of fear is central in a number of political philosophies, not least those of Machiavelli and Hobbes, and in chapter Six I look at the role of fear as a basis for political philosophy as well as the political use that has been made of fear in the 'war against terror' of recent years. Finally, the concluding chapter asks if there is any way out of fear, if we can break down the climate of fear that surrounds us today.

A theme that will only be dealt with to a slight extent is the fear of death in general, as this is such a wide-ranging theme – because it calls for a thorough thematization of our conceptions of death – and must therefore be dealt with elsewhere. Anxiety – or *Angst* – will also be dealt with just as briefly. An obvious question is: Why write a 'philosophy of fear' when it is not so much fear as anxiety that has been traditionally dealt with in philosophy? Since anxiety is in addition ascribed major metaphysical implications, fear would seem to be trivial by comparison. Anxiety is 'deep', whereas fear is 'shallow'. In Roland Barthes' words we can say that fear would appear to be a 'mediocre and unworthy emotion'.[1] Nevertheless, fear would seem today to have greater cultural and political consequences than anxiety. Furthermore, it is basically rather pleasant to do away with all the 'metaphysical hand-luggage' that accompanies the concept of anxiety.

My thanks to Anne Granberg, Helge Jordheim, Ingrid Sande Larsen, Thomas Sevenius Nilsen, Erik Thorstensen, Ingrid Ugelvik and Knut Olav Åmås for their comments on the text. All errors, inaccuracies and fallacies still remaining are solely my responsibility.

ONE

The Culture of Fear

Quite an experience, to live in fear, isn't it?
That's what it is to be a slave.
The replicant Roy Batty in *Blade Runner* (1982)

Oh Baby, here comes the fear again.
The end is near again.
Pulp: 'The Fear', *This is Hardcore* (1998)

It has become something of an ordeal to get through security at an airport. It can fill you with nostalgia to think back to the time, only a few years ago, when you could more or less walk straight through, once you had emptied your pockets of coins and keys. When travelling, I often return on the same day, so I have no other luggage than a book or two and some papers in a bag. But I always have one object with me that is clearly considered a security risk: a lighter. So I have to take it out of my pocket, place it in a transparent plastic bag and send it through separately before I can take it out of the plastic bag once more and return it to my pocket. On longer trips, where you also need to have such things with you as toothpaste, deodorant and shampoo, everything that broadly can be classified as 'fluids' has to be packed in a transparent plastic bag that may not contain more than one litre, with no individual container exceeding 100 ml. Should you have a half-empty bottle of shampoo with you that can when full contain 150 ml of liquid, it must be left outside the security control. And you can of course forget everything about taking a bottle of water or wine with you.

These new regulations are the result of terrorist plans, which were discovered in London in autumn 2006, to use liquid explosives to blow up planes. The regulations – which restrict the freedom of millions of passengers every year – are, in other words, justified by a terror attack that did *not* take place. Passengers have, however, accepted this restriction of their freedom without any protests worth mentioning. The fear of terror functions here as a kind of trump card, one that wins over all other considerations.

This is just one example among many as to how fear is shaping our space of action. Fear would seem to have become all-embracing, in the sense that there is no longer any area of society left where a perspective of fear does not apply. Fear has become the emotion that controls the public, and a number of social scientists now claim that today's society can best be described as a 'culture of fear'.[1] Fear has become a culturally determined magnifying glass through which we consider the world.

In *Tractatus logico-philosophicus*, Ludwig Wittgenstein writes: 'the world of the happy man is different from that of the unhappy man.'[2] Twisting Wittengenstein's formulation a bit, we could write: the world of the secure man is different from that of the fearful man. Jean-Paul Sartre emphasizes this point: 'An emotion totally changes the world.'[3] The secure person lives in a reliable world – the word 'secure' means 'untroubled by feelings of fear, doubt or vulnerability' – while the insecure person lives in a world that at any time can turn against him, where the basis of existence at any time can be pulled out from under his feet. Dangers threaten us everywhere: in dark streets and inside our homes, with strangers and with those closest to us, in nature as well as in technology, inside our bodies as well as in external forces. There no longer seems to be anything that is really secure.

In fear we are met by something outside ourselves, and what we meet is a negation of what we want. We fear the important things in life being destroyed or taken away from us, such as our freedom, dignity, health, social status and – taken to its extreme – our lives. We fear not only for ourselves but also for others, and especially those dear to us. When any of this is threatened, fear is a normal reaction. We want to protect ourselves against such threats. For human life *is* frightening. As Montaigne says: 'Our human frailty means that we have more to flee from than to strive for.'[4] There appears to be something fundamental about fear, and it is scarcely a coincidence that fear is the first emotion to be mentioned in the Bible: when Adam ate from the Tree of Knowledge and discovered that he was naked, fear preceded shame.[5] We are born into the world naked and unarmed, and – compared to most other animals – remain in this defenceless state for the rest of our lives.

Even so, it is not evident that this is the most appropriate perspective on human life. It can be claimed that all aware-ness of – or obsession with – risk is a greater danger than all the risks that otherwise exist.[6] My point is not that we live in a world without dangers. It would seem to be clear, for example, that global warming may have highly dramatic consequences for the entire planet. In most cities of a certain size one ought to avoid certain locations at certain times of the day or night because the danger of being assaulted is great. And one ought to look both ways before crossing the road. There are a range of phenomena we ought to fear. The problem is that we seem to see *everything* from a perspective of fear.

If we do a search through a British newspaper archive, we find a marked increase in the phrase 'at risk' over the last decade, from 2,037 occurrences in 1994 to 18,003 in 2000.[7] In the Norwegian newspaper database *a-text*, we find a marked increase in the incidence of the Norwegian word for fear over the past decade, from 3,331 uses in 1996 to 5,883 in 2006.[8] It is tempting to explain the increase by, among other things, the terror attacks of 9/11, but an interesting feature is that the increase started well *before* these attacks. Viewed thus, we can assert that the terror attacks not only increased the awareness of fear but also fitted into an already existing pattern – and that increase has continued to the present day. These figures indicate that the media are constantly reminding us about how 'dangerous' the world is – and not least how afraid we are of it.

The same picture is confirmed by a number of other surveys. For example, Norstat carried out a survey in 2005 for Siemens, which supplies safety equipment, in which 1,000 subjects were asked if, over recent years, they had become more afraid of experiencing various phenomena. The result was that 51% had become more afraid of experiencing violent crime, 47% traffic accidents, 36% acts of terror, 26% fires and 19% natural disasters.[9] The increase, by the way, was larger for women than for men.

We believe that the earth, air and water are becoming increasingly polluted, that crime is constantly increasing, that our food is becoming increasingly full of harmful additives and pollutants. We imagine that we are becoming increasingly exposed to all types of dangers and that the dangers are becoming more frequent and more acute. In a survey in which people were asked to assess a wide range of 90 potentially dangerous activities or objects, from jogging and cosmetics to terrorism and vaccines, only 25 were thought to be decreasing in dangerousness, while no less than 62 were thought to be increasing in danger – and 13 of these markedly so.[10] Most risk analysts would claim that the level of danger in most of the phenomena included in the survey has actually considerably declined. The results of this survey are by no means an anomaly – on the contrary, there is a prevalent perception among most people that we are exposed to greater risk today than previously, and that things will get even worse in the future.[11]

Fear is also contagious. If someone becomes afraid of something, this fear has a tendency to spread to others, who in turn spread it further. This may occur even though there was initially no rational basis for the fear.[12] If many people fear something, we cannot deduce that this phenomenon actually *is* something to fear.

Risk awareness has even become fashionable: 'paranoia chic' is a new trend.[13] Bullet-proof clothing with a fashionable cut is apparently very popular.[14] In 2005–6 the Museum of Modern Art in New York put on the exhibition *Safe: Design Takes on Risk*, where all sorts of objects that can protect us in one way or another were displayed as examples of cutting-edge design. The exhibition catalogue states: 'Today, the simple need of protection has mutated into the complex universe we call fashion.'[15] The curator emphasized fear as a source of creativity: 'Especially in everyday life, security is an industry in constant expansion, because, since there is no end to what could go wrong, there is also no end to the creative and commercial possibilities design can offer.'[16] The moral of the exhibition is: 'Good design, combined with good instinct, is our strongest assurance of progress toward a safer, more liveable world.'[17] Fear has also become a theme in architecture, where an important element of the function of a building is to protect inhabitants and users against something threatening 'out there'.[18]

We seem to be obsessed with every conceivable danger. Not only do we fear dangers; they are also good entertainment. One example is the British television series *So You Think You're Safe?* The series deals with the hidden dangers of everyday life, and stresses all the accidents that can befall modern man in the course of a completely normal day. It is the perfect programme for the postmodern paranoiac. For a paranoiac with a hint of self-irony, *I'm Afraid, You're Afraid: 448 Things to Fear and Why* (2000) can be recommended – a sort of mini-encyclopaedia of everything that is dangerous in everyday life.[19] In recent years, a series of books have appeared that assert that various global disasters are imminent. Among the most popular are such books as Jared

Diamond's *Collapse: How Societies Choose to Fail or Succeed*, James Howard Kunstler's *The Long Emergency: Surviving the End of Oil, Climate Change, and Other Converging Catastrophes of the Twenty-First Century* and Eugene Linden's *The Winds of Change: Climate, Weather and the Destruction of Civilizations*.[20] In addition, there are self-help books on what one ought to do when the disaster actually strikes, such as Matthew Stein's *When Technology Fails: A Manual for Self-Reliance and Planetary Survival* and Jack A. Spigarelli's *Crisis Preparedness Handbook: A Complete Guide to Home Storage and Physical Survival*.[21] On the basis of these books, one is tempted to believe that the Apocalypse is just around the corner.

Fear is not least an important political resource for public authorities, political parties and pressure groups. In an age where the old ideologies no longer have such strong powers of motivation, fear becomes one of the most powerful agents in the political discourse. Fear paves the way for being able to communicate a message and it can be used to undermine one's opponents and the imminent danger of their being in power. Discussions of modern politics or politicial candidates often just explore which risk ought to worry us most.

Here these political players exist in a perfect symbiosis with the mass media, since scaring people undoubtedly sells newspapers and attracts people to TV screens – it is for this reason that TV news and newspapers often seem to be in competition with each other to report the biggest scares. The entertainment industry has also joined in. A film like *The Day After Tomorrow* (2004) was embraced by many environmental activists because it had the 'right' message, despite the fact that from a scientific point of view it managed to get most things wrong concerning global warming, apart from the somewhat obvious fact that we are facing a serious environmental problem.

In *The End is Nigh*, a book about natural disasters, the geologist Henrik Svensen writes: 'If we look at what lies ahead, natural disasters are going to become even more frequent. Man-made climate changes and global warming will lead to more extreme weather. Hurricanes *can* become more violent, landslides more frequent, inundations more destructive and periods of drought longer.'[22] In the following sentences it is then stated that natural disasters *can* and *will* become worse, but there is a huge difference between stating a hypothetical possibility that something may happen and a certainty that it will actually do so. There is a shift between possibility and reality – and as long as one is in the realm of possibilities, all disasters are within reach.

Most things would, of course, indicate that climate changes really ought to worry us, but the same is hardly the case for the innumerable other dangers that we encounter everyday in the news picture. Anything can be presented as being dangerous insofar as information is put forward in a sufficiently one-sided way.[23] The mass media often do not ask questions about information coming from idealistic organizations, despite the fact that these undoubtedly have an agenda and often present information in a way that is far from balanced.[24] Not everyone adopts the fears that are promoted by various pressure groups, but many people accept unquestioningly the assertions made without investigating their viability more closely.

A recurring feature is that *potential* dangers are presented as if they were *actual* dangers. The world is full of potential dangers. Someone may push you in front of a train, you may have a meteorite land on your head and a terrorist may hijack the plane you are sitting in, but it is hardly a good idea to base your everyday life on such things happening. Most potential dangers never become actual ones.

All ages have had their own fear, but what fear is changes. Today, there are hardly as many people in our part of the world who fear eternal perdition, but all the more who fear cancer, terrorism and eco-disasters. A British survey claims that half of the country's 11-year-olds often lie awake at night because they are worried about climate change.[25] When I was growing up, the nuclear threat was the most powerful source of apocalyptic fear. I probably belong to the last – or at least provisionally the last – generation that grew up in the belief that there was an imminent danger of a nuclear war that could lead to the extermination of the human race. Expressions such as 'nuclear winter' were part of our imagined future. In 1983 more than half of all British teenagers believed that a nuclear war would take place in their own lifetime.[26] Nuclear weapons are still a threat, but it is not the great, overriding threat in most people's consciousnesses, even though some people stress nuclear weapons in the hands of terrorists as a particularly worrying scenario.[27] Instead, nuclear weapons are more just a part of a larger weapons arsenal and they occur less in the form of long-distance rockets than small bombs that can be contained in a suitcase. For it is very frightening that a small plastic bag can be pierced and allow sarin to escape in a metro carriage,[28] or that anthrax bacteria can be sent in an ordinary envelope. The question is what role such a fear ought to be allowed to play in our lives.

'The terrorist' is perhaps the most threatening figure in today's world. Of course, terrorism is no new phenomenon, but it is perfectly adapted to a globalized world that is already prepared to fear most things. It can in principle strike at any time and any place; we are not safe anywhere. The probability of being killed in a terrorist attack is, however, microscopic – something I will return to in chapter Six.

If we look at the state of the world as a whole, the situation is better than it has been for a long time. There are fewer civil wars, genocides and breaches of human rights than there have ever been.[29] All statistics indicate that we in the

West in particular are living in the most secure societies that have ever existed, where the dangers are fewer and our chance of dealing with them greater than ever before. We must after all lead a highly protected life to have the time to fear all the potential dangers that may strike us. Fear begins with our fearing this and that, but with a sufficient number of repetitions and a spreading out to ever more phenomena it can become a general perspective on life. In a culture that in many ways is characterized by social disintegration, fear is something we all share, a unifying perspective on existence. Fear has become a basic characteristic of our entire culture. As the British sociologist Frank Furedi writes: 'Western societies are increasingly dominated by a culture of fear. The defining feature of this culture is the belief that humanity is confronted by powerful destructive forces that threaten our everyday existence.'[30] We are regularly confronted with the idea that 'the end is near', whether we are dealing with GM food or bird flu. In addition, dangers are stressed in absolutely every activity a human life might possibly contain.

Fear is undoubtedly an important sales tool for the mass media, and it is being given more and more space.[31] The mass media help create a fear that is out of proportion to the facts. They bombard us with tales of mortally dangerous viruses, terrorists, paedophile teachers, violent teenagers, eco-disasters and poisonous food. It is tempting to say that the media play so pivotal a role that a danger or catastrophe becomes 'real' only when it gets press coverage. People who watch a lot of TV are more inclined than others to perceive their neighbourhood as insecure, to believe that crime is on the increase and that they are in danger.[32]

The logic of the mass media is one of the most important causes of the growth of the culture of fear, but it is at the same time obvious that this culture has only been able to develop because we are susceptible to this form of logic.

Seen from a natural perspective, humans are highly exposed creatures. We are born into a world we cannot control, and seem to be consigned to existential uncertainty throughout our lives. Our fear, however, seems to be to an ever decreasing extent to be based on our own experiences. How many of us have been exposed to a terrorist attack, violence from strangers, been seriously ill as a result of food additives or a new virus? The answer is, extremely few of us. Most of us live until we are 70–80 years old and die of old age, without having been seriously affected by any of this. We live lives that are so protected that we can focus our attention on a series of potential dangers that, as far as can be ascertained, will never be realized in our lives. Our fear is a by-product of luxury. But that does not make it any less real.

TWO

What is Fear?

Dolendi modus, timendi non item.
(To suffering there is a limit; to fearing, none.)
Francis Bacon: 'Of Seditions and Troubles', *Essays* (1625)

The reason why fear has emerged as an evolutionary phenomenon is quite evident: a creature without the capacity to feel fear will have a worse chance of surviving and procreating. It is obvious that fear can often be of great assistance to us. It increases our readiness and can thus help us out of dangerous situations or prevent our ever landing up in them. Fear not only protects us from predatory animals and other dangers that exist in nature but also from many self-initiated dangers, like walking straight out into heavy traffic without looking. Fear contributes to keeping us alive. But fear can also become dysfunctional. It does so when a disparity arises between fear and its object, or when it causes us to 'lose our heads'. Before examining in more detail at what attitude we ought to adopt to fear, we ought to look more closely at what kind of a phenomenon fear really is. I intend to use a range of approaches from neurophysiology to phenomenology, and will end up with a perception of fear that to a great extent can be described as a culturally conditioned *habit*.

To be able to answer the question 'What is fear?' we ought perhaps also to answer the question of what an emotion is in general. That is not so simple. 'Emotion' is a term that can cover a range of highly dissimilar phenomena – from pain, hunger and thirst to pride, envy and love, from the almost purely physiological to the almost completely cognitive. We can see that the first-named emotions are more 'physical' while the last-named are more 'mental' entities. In English a distinction is made between 'feelings' and 'emotions', where

21

the first-named are more 'feelings' and the last-named more 'emotions'. It should, however, be pointed out that there still is considerable disagreement as to where exactly one is to draw the dividing line between 'feelings' and 'emotions' and what states belong to the one term or the other.

I do not intend to write all that much about emotions in general in this chapter, but move on fairly directly to fear, although certain basic points and theories must be touched on even so.[1] The social anthropologist Paul Ekman argues for the existence of a set of basic emotions, that is, ones found in all cultures and ones that are not acquired but innate.[2] We can find a similar thought expressed by Descartes. Many people support such a concept, but there is disagreement as to how many such emotions exist and what they are. Most people normally include anger, fear, joy, disgust and surprise, but there is no consensus. In an overview of fourteen lists of 'basic emotions' it is striking that there is not one single emotion that is included in all lists.[3] Even if we could assume that such a set of basic emotions exists, we have not necessarily come any closer to an understanding of them, because these emotions can be expressed in quite different ways in different cultural contexts.[4] Cultural norms seem to be crucial in determining which emotions are expressed and to what extent.

Emotions are often viewed as being purely internal, accessible only via a kind of introspection on the part of the person who feels them. They are, however, not simply concealed, purely mental entities but also behaviour, actions and expressions that are visible from the outside. They exist in facial expressions and gestures and are not concealed behind them. Emotions are a way of being present in the world, a way of getting a grip on it and acting in it. Given that emotions cannot be separated from expressions of emotion, and that the latter actually vary quite a bit from culture to culture, it also follows that emotions are culture-relative.

The phenomenologist Maurice Merleau-Ponty maintains that there is a strong link between an emotion and the physical expression of it. He stresses that the emotion is not something that lies behind or beneath a gesture but is contained in – or *is* – the gesture:

> Faced with an angry or threatening gesture, I have no need, in order to understand it, to recall the feelings which I myself experienced when I used these gestures on my own account. I know very little, from inside, of the mime of anger so that a decisive factor is missing for any association by resemblance or reasoning by analogy, and what is more, I do not see anger or a threatening attitude as a psychic fact hidden behind the gesture, I read anger in it. The gesture does not make me think of anger, it is anger itself.[5]

This does not mean of course that we would be unable to conceal an emotion, or that a concealed emotion is not 'real', but rather that the concealed emotion presupposes the explicit one. Merleau-Ponty considers emotions, their expression and the relations between them as flexible. He claims that the expression of different emotions varies from culture to culture:

> The fact is that the behaviour associated with anger or love is not the same in a Japanese and an Occidental. Or, to be more precise, the difference in behaviour corresponds to a difference in the emotions themselves. It is not only the gesture which is contingent in relation to the body's organisation, it is the manner itself in which we meet the situation and live it.[6]

As he sees it, it is impossible to distinguish between a 'natural' and 'conventional' level in emotions and their expression in human beings – the natural and the conventional overlap seamlessly. There are reasons for believing that Merleau-Ponty is exaggerating the randomness of emotions and their expression – but he does have a point.

Several emotions are fairly similar in how they are physiologically expressed. In investigations where people were asked to identify other people's emotions from photographs, most people managed to identify happy, sad and angry faces, while considerably fewer were able to identify frightened faces, which were often confused with anger, suspicion and surprise.[7] These emotions are normally fairly distinct when subjectively experienced, though it must be admitted that, for example, anger often contains an element of fear.

It is tremendously difficult to distinguish clearly between biological, physiological and social aspects in emotions. Even though the emotions undoubtedly have a biological basis, it is clear that they are also shaped by both individual experiences and social norms. Emotions have an evolutionary, a social and a personal history, and if we are to understand them, we must take all three into account. Emotions are not simply something 'natural' and direct; they are also social constructs.[8] The norms for when it is suitable to have and to show a given emotion vary from culture to culture – and also with social status. The ability to learn language is another example of a universally human phenomenon and it too has a biological basis, but the semantic resources vary even so from culture to culture and from individual to individual. The same would seem to apply to emotions. What we fear, and how strongly, depends on our conceptions of the world, of what dangerous forces exist in it and what possibilities we have of protecting ourselves against them. Our knowledge and experience of emotions are not independent of the social context in which they occur.

One approach in seeking to understand emotions is to use their biochemical aspects as a point of departure. It is, however, difficult to distinguish between fear and several other emotions biochemically – fear and anger, for example, have extremely similar biochemical components.[9] As we shall see later, there is no definite physical state that is a necessary or a sufficient condition for an emotional state: two people can be in the same physical state but have different emotional states, or they can be in the same emotional state but have different physical states. Variants of one and the same basic emotion can have different physical correlations in the same person at different times. Another problem about seeking to identify fear from its biochemistry is that different fears seem to have different biochemical correlations – a person who is afraid of being exposed to an act of violence will normally have a high level of adrenaline, whereas a person who is afraid of contracting an illness will normally not have raised adrenaline levels.

There are physical reactions that are often connected with fear, for example, breathing and heartbeat become quicker and one trembles, or all movements 'freeze'. Rats and humans have a very similar physiology here, in that the amygdala – the brain's centre for emotions – is stimulated and sends signals to the hypothalamus and the pituitary gland, which then causes stress hormones to be released from the adrenal glands. As in other animals, our brains react to threats by releasing substances such as adrenaline and cortisol in large quantities, discharging the nervous system faster and dilating the pupils. The amygdala sends signals so quickly that they overwhelm us before we have any chance of intervening rationally.

There is quite simply very little that human reason can do when fear sets in. Montaigne emphasizes that this applies even to the person most governed by reason, namely, the philosopher:

> The philosopher must shut his eyes against the blow that threatens him; he must tremble upon the margin of a

precipice, like a child; nature having reserved these light marks of her authority, not to be forced by our reason and the stoic virtue, to teach man his mortality and our weakness.[10]

David Hume underlines that even the evils that we are scarcely able to imagine happening, because the likelihood of them happening is so infinitesimally small, can arouse fear.[11] Not only that, he continues, but we can even be overwhelmed by a fear of evils that we know to be impossible, such as the fear of falling from a great height when we are in complete safety on a ledge.

You cannot easily remove fear by an act of will, but you can moderate fear chemically by using medication or by getting used to the feared object over time. A sure cure for fear is to put the amygdala out of action, since people with damage to the amygdala are unable to feel fear, even in life-threatening situations.[12] Nor are they capable of discerning fear in the faces of others.[13] For anyone with a functional amygdala, fear is difficult to stop once it comes. You cannot quite simply decide not to be afraid, since rationality in such cases is 'steamrollered' by the amygdala, but you can, as mentioned, practise changing your reaction pattern over a period of time.

The American neurophysiologist Joseph LeDoux believes he has shown that fear is controlled by two distinct neural paths in the brain.[14] One of these provides a very swift response, but it also has a tendency to be over-sensitive and often it releases a 'false alarm'. The other one is slower, but takes a larger amount of information into account, and this one can stop the first fear response when there does not seem to be any basis for it. It must be stressed, however, that this second response is also a physical phenomenon – we are not dealing with a subject consciously stopping a fear response. Someone who has been badly scared on one occasion by an event or an object will also be more easily scared by the same thing on later occasions. It seems that when being repeatedly exposed to experiences that provoke fear, the organs involved actually grow, so that one is in fact training the organism's ability to feel fear.[15] This may ultimately result in an organism in a chronic state of fear or anxiety.

The problem with such approaches as that of LeDoux is that they do not take the cultural aspects of our emotional life into consideration. He is basically uninterested in the existence of emotions apart from the purely physiological level, because states of the brain and bodily reactions are considered to be what is fundamental, with conscious emotions being considered only as surface phenomena by comparison.[16] This, however, is to overlook everything that distinguishes human emotional life from what we find in other animals. We would support the claim of the philosopher Michael Meyers when he says that passion is 'the unique but enigmatic locus wherein people meet animals, and human nature encounters nature'.[17] Exclusively focusing on the 'animal' aspects of human emotional life, as people as LeDoux do, cannot solve this mystery. The relationship between human fear and what we find in other animals is a hotly debated subject. It is, for example, paradoxical that fear in rats is a non-cognitive entity (since it is completely unconnected to rational considerations, because rats do not possess such skills), while it is cognitive in humans – and yet we still feel able to talk about the same feeling in rats and humans.[18] I have no ambitions about launching some solution to that paradox here.

Biologically speaking, we are to a great extent equipped with the same apparatus for feeling fear as other animals, but our cognitive, linguistic and symbolical skills provide us with a completely different register of emotion. A hare does not fear a predator that is located on some other continent, and it is scarcely worried by there being residues of pesticides in the food it eats. The hare's fear is a result of what is in its vicinity, here and now. It is not first and foremost physiology that distinguishes human fear from what other animals experience, but rather what is capable of arousing fear. Aristotle writes: 'plainly the things we fear are terrible things, and these are, to speak without qualification, evils; for which reason people even define fear as expectation of evil. Now we fear all evils, e.g. disgrace, poverty, disease, friendlessness, death.'[19] Everything mentioned by Aristotle is hardly feared by any other creature than man. Human fear would seem, then, to differ essentially from what we find in other animals. Martin Heidegger takes this point to its logical extreme when he claims that only the sort of beings who can relate to their own being can fear, from which it follows that fear becomes something that exists only in human life.[20] This is undoubtedly an exaggeration, since there is also a strong continuity between what we call fear in humans and a similar state in animals.

The Aristotelian definition of man is *zoon logon echon*. This is often translated as 'rational animal', but it can also be rendered as 'life that possesses language'. Man has linguistic and symbolical resources that other animals do not possess. The capacity to form symbols grants us a certain degree of independence in relation to the world, as we can replace objects by symbols for those objects. The philosopher Ernst Cassirer writes:

> Man cannot escape from his own achievement. He cannot but adopt the conditions of his own life. No longer in a merely physical universe, man lives in a symbolic universe. Language, myth, art, and religion are parts of this universe. They are the varied threads which weave the symbolic net, the tangled web of human experience. All human progress in thought and experience refines upon and strengthens this net. No longer can man confront

reality immediately; he cannot see it, as it were, face to face. Physical reality seems to recede in proportion as man's symbolic activity advances. Instead of dealing with the things themselves man is in a sense constantly conversing with himself. He has so enveloped himself in linguistic forms, in artistic images, in mythical symbols or religious rites that he cannot see or know anything except by the interposition of this artificial medium. His situation is the same in the theoretical as in the practical sphere. Even here man does not live in a world of hard facts, or according to his immediate needs and desires. He lives rather in the midst of imaginary emotions, in hopes and fears, in illusions and disillusions, in his fantasies and dreams. 'What disturbs and alarms man,' said Epictetus, 'are not the things, but his opinions and fancies about the things.'[21]

We humans can fear most things. Our fear has a much greater potential scope than the fear any other animal can feel, precisely because we are an *animal symbolicum*. As soon as we hear of a danger, no matter how distant, we often perceive it as a threat to ourselves. Not least, we construct innumerable imaginary threats – and here we find an important cause of the atrocities humans commit against each other. As Ernest Becker writes:

[M]en are truly sorry creatures because they have made death conscious. They can see evil in anything that wounds them, causes ill health, or even deprives them of pleasure. Consciousness means too that they have to be preoccupied with evil even in the absence of any immediate danger. Their lives become a meditation on evil and a planned venture for controlling it and forestalling it. The result is one of the great tragedies of human existence, what we might call the need to 'fetishize evil', to locate the threat to life in some special places where it can be placated and controlled. It is tragic precisely because it is sometimes very arbitrary: men make fantasies about evil, see it in the wrong places, and destroy themselves and others by uselessly thrashing about.[22]

Fear can undoubtedly motivate attacks. This is an important point in Thucydides' explanation as to why the Peloponnesian war broke out: the Spartans were afraid because the Athenians were becoming much too powerful, and therefore constituted an ever greater threat.[23]

Emotions are closely linked to specific patterns of action, and it seems that these patterns of action have developed because they have been favourable from an evolutionary point of view.[24] Fear is typically accompanied by flight or attack. But not always. Many emotions are of such a nature that it is vital *not* to express them in any way. The title of a song by Morrissey is 'We Hate it When our Friends Become Successful', and this may at times be true. Envy, not least that of one's friends, is, however, among the least sympathetic traits of a human's emotional life, and the envious person would do wisely to conceal it as well as possible. As François de La Rochefoucauld points out: 'People are often vain of their passions, even of the worst, but envy is a passion so timid and shame-faced that no one ever dare avow her.'[25] All of us have presumably experienced being hopelessly in love with another person without revealing it by so much as a facial expression or gesture because so much is at stake. Or being in a dangerous situation where one feels fear like a fist to the stomach, but understands at the same time that one simply cannot allow oneself to show fear because the situation will then just get worse. It would be unreasonable to claim that one does not have the emotion in question in such situations simply because one does not express the emotion via a particular action. Emotions *motivate* action, but they do not determine it.

Fear often motivates flight, but it can also be so over-whelming that one is completely incapable of action. Lucretius describes this in *On the Nature of Things*:

> But when the mind is moved by shock more fierce,
> We mark the whole soul suffering all at once
> Along man's members: sweats and pallors spread
> Over the body, and the tongue is broken,
> And fails the voice away, and ring the ears,
> Mists blind the eyeballs, and the joints collapse,
> – Aye, men drop dead from terror of the mind.[26]

The person who fears will normally attempt to escape or avoid what he believes is threatening his life, health or inter-ests. The typical pattern of action for fear is thus flight, to attempt to create the greatest possible distance from the feared object, to get outside the range of danger. Flight need not be understood spatially, that is, it is not necessarily a question of running away; it can just as well consist of cre-ating a barrier between oneself and the object, such as pro-tecting oneself with one's arms or hiding behind a door. The crucial thing is that in some way or other one tries to posi-tion oneself where one is invulnerable.

We usually think of bodily reactions being followed by an experienced emotion. A theory that reverses this picture is normally called the James-Lange theory, after the philosopher William James and the physiologist and psy-chologist Carl Georg Lange. There are certain differences between James's and Lange's theories, which were devel-oped independently of each other, but the basic idea is the same: that it is not the emotion that causes the physical change, but the opposite. You do not cry because you are sad, but are sad because you cry.[27] Similarly, you do not flee a danger because you are afraid – you are afraid because you flee a danger.

In 1927 the physiologist W. B. Cannon criticized the James-Lange theory, pointing out that the same physiological changes take place in connection with highly different emotional and also non-emotional states.[28] He also demonstrated that humans may have a form of behaviour that corresponds to what is normal when one has a given emotion, and that they also report that they have this emotion, and yet they do not have the physiological state that is normally associated with that emotion. Nor have later experiments managed to establish a necessary link between an emotional and a physiological state.

The physical feeling of being harassed is not in itself sufficient to tell me to what extent. For example, I am in a state of fear, anger or sorrow. For it to be able to be identified as a particular mental emotion, something more is needed. In the early 1960s the psychologists Stanley Schachter and Jerome Singer advanced a hypothesis that included elements of the theories of both James-Lange and Cannon.[29] Their theory of so-called *cognitive labelling* says that both physical changes and a cognitive interpretation of these are necessary for one to experience a given emotion. According to this theory, a person will experience anger by noticing that the heart beats faster, that breathing becomes quicker, etc., and then interpreting the situation as one where anger would be an adequate response. The same applies to fear. To what extent an emotion is identified as fear or anger would thus seem to depend on the situation, or rather, it depends on how a person interprets the situation in which he finds himself. Two people who are in the same situation and in the same physical (biochemical) state can identify the emotion they have as fear and anger respectively, depending on their interpretation of the situation. And both of them may, of course, be right. An emotion is *not* something independent of the situation in which it takes place and the person's interpretation.

A problem with the theory of *cognitive labelling* is that it would seem to presume that there is always a particular sequence of events, where the 'physical' change or feeling comes first, and that this then becomes a 'mental' emotion because of a given interpretation. But is it not possible to say that the interpretation often comes first and the emotion follows the interpretation, that one interprets a given situation in a particular way – for example, that this is a situation where I normally ought to feel anger, jealousy or fear – and then the emotion comes?

One's conceptions and interpretations would seem to be crucial for the identification of one's emotions. At the same time, they do not seem to be completely determinative, because one's conceptions of an object can change, while the emotion regarding the object remains the same. As a child I believed that spiders were dangerous, and was terribly afraid of them, especially after my brother was once badly bitten by one. Later, I learned that most spiders are fairly harmless – at least in our part of the world – but the fear of them nevertheless remained. It has diminished over the years, but I do not believe I will ever be completely free of my arachnophobia. A person can be afraid of flying, even though he is convinced that flying is an extremely safe way to travel. This would seem to contradict the theory that one's conceptions are crucial for one's emotions, since the conceptions of the object and one's emotions regarding the object are pulling in opposite directions. My mother has always reacted to mice by leaping up onto the dining table and screaming – just as in innumerable cartoons. She does not, however, believe that the mouse is capable of harming her. She has basically never believed that. Even so, it would be unreasonable to claim that she is not in a state of fear just because she is not convinced that the mouse will harm her. This is a problem for the cognitive theory.

A possible solution to the problem could be that one has not completely replaced former conceptions by new ones, but rather has contradictory conceptions, that is, that the opposition is not between a conception and an emotion but between two conceptions, where one of them has the decisive influence on the emotions.[30] In fact, we often have contradictory conceptions, where we believe A and not-A, for example, when we rationally believe to have done away with a conception (for instance, that flying is dangerous), but it nevertheless continues to apply.

Furthermore, we may be wrong about our own emotions.[31] Our emotions are so strongly influenced by our conceptions that all of us have experienced believing that in a given situation we have emotion x, but gradually discover that it is more a question of emotion y. The self is not completely transparent to itself, and we may deceive ourselves when it comes to our emotions, for example, because we are unwilling to acknowledge that an emotion underlying a particular action is an unsuitable one. Even though we are occasionally wrong about our emotions, this does not mean that we usually are. For to be able to talk at all about errors in such a context presupposes that we generally identify our emotions correctly – otherwise it would not make sense to talk about 'errors'.

Emotions seem to provide knowledge about the world. Or rather, without emotions there is much we are unable to perceive about the world. An emotion contains conceptions. These conceptions do not deal only with physical relations – for example, a polar bear starts coming towards me when I am walking around the North Pole – but also evaluations: this polar bear is a danger to me. My pulse begins to race, my breathing grows quicker and I start to tremble slightly. There is nothing about these physical changes alone that indicate it is precisely fear I am feeling right now, because other emotional states can be accompanied by exactly the same physical phenomena – sexual ecstasy, for example. What makes my emotion in this situation one of fear is my perception of being in a dangerous situation. But I would not have been able to experience the situation as being dangerous either without the capacity to feel fear.

Fear always has an intentional object. It is always directed at something. Without such an object we would not be dealing with fear, only heart palpitations, quick breathing and trembling. Fear is something more than these physical states, and this 'more' is the intentional object. The intentional object has always already been interpreted. What distinguishes fear from anger, sorrow or joy is not the object in itself but the interpretation of it. One and the same object can be interpreted in such a way that it gives rise to all the named emotions. If I interpret the object as threatening, I feel fear, while an interpretation of it as being annoying can lead to anger, etc. For fear to announce itself, the threat must be perceived as being serious. I must also believe that the danger cannot easily be averted.

One can of course be in a state that resembles fear without being able to say what it is one fears. It is then possible that one ought rather to describe the state as anxiety. Fear and anxiety are closely related states. Both contain the idea of a danger or possibly injury. This threat can, however, be quite specific, or something less precise. A usual distinction between fear and anxiety is precisely that fear has a specific object whereas anxiety lacks this. This distinction is normally connected with Kierkegaard and Heidegger, but we find a precursor for it in Kant: 'Fear of an object that threatens with some indefinite evil is *anxiety*.'[32] The crucial thing here is the indefinite nature of the fear. If you ask a person in a state of fear what he or she fears, the person in question can, broadly speaking, give you quite a clear answer. And if you ask him what he desires in this situation, he can, broadly speaking, answer this as well – for the feared object to disappear, for him to be protected against it, or something similar. The person suffering from anxiety, on the other hand, will not be able to give any clear answer to either of these questions.

It must be admitted, however, that the dividing line between anxiety and fear is not, in practice, as clear as these conceptual distinctions maybe imply. First, fear can also contain uncertainty as regards both its object and possible ways out: you fear a particular object, but do not know for sure what it is about the object that you fear, or what attitude you would like to adopt to the object. Many anxiety afflictions are also characterized by having an object, that one knows what one is anxious about, but where it is uncertain how the object is going to manifest itself in one's life. Precisely how one ought to – or is at all able to – draw an absolute distinction between fear and anxiety is not going to be discussed further here, and I have chosen to stick to the traditional distinction between the two, as being object-specific and objectless respectively.

When we say that fear always has an intentional object, this does not mean that it always has a *real* object. Most of us presumably feared some monster or other as a child – whether we believed it hid in the cupboard or under the bed. When young, I believed that there was a ghost in the shower outside my parents' bedroom and, without a doubt, it was eerie, since I had to go through the bathroom to get to my parents at night when the world seemed sinister. Even though there in reality was no monster in the cupboard, under the bed or in the bathroom, this does not mean that this fear was without an object – the object was precisely the monster that I imagined existed in those places. When I am at the cinema and am frightened in a film by a character, it is not because I believe that this character actually exists.[33] I am able to distinguish between fantasy and reality, and am perfectly well aware that the frightening character is fictive. And my fear has an intentional object – the fictive character.

What about a fear of 'the unknown'? The writer Elias Canetti writes: 'There is nothing that man fears more than to be affected by something unknown. One wants to see what is reaching out for one, one wants to identify it or at least place it in a context.'[34] Similarly, H. P. Lovecraft begins his classic essay on fear and the supernatural with the words: 'The oldest and strongest human emotion is fear, and the oldest and strongest form of fear is the fear of the unknown.'[35] Such a fear of 'the unknown' is not an objectless fear. Rather, the object of fear here is indefinite, but is still very much a fear of *something*. It is a fear that something unpleasant or frightening can occur.

Certain emotions are normally assumed to tell us something about reality. Fear is one of these. It is then considered to be an instrument of perception. All such instruments, however, can function adequately or inadequately. We have seen that a person's interpretation of a situation is crucial for the person's emotions regarding that situation. Some interpretations, however, are inadequate, and they will lead to our emotional judgement of a situation also becoming inadequate. As Aristotle points out, we make errors when we fear the wrong things, in the wrong ways or at the wrong times.[36] If, for example, I am afraid of flying but not of driving a car, because I (erroneously) believe it is more dangerous to fly than to drive a car, the emotion will be wrong. I can also feel too much fear in relation to an object that there actually is a certain danger attached to, but where this fear does not have any reasonable relation to the danger. For most people, this has an intuitive appeal. Most people seem to believe that an emotion like fear can be rationally evaluated, that a feeling of fear can be right or wrong. A feeling of fear gives adequate perception if its object is dangerous, and there is a reasonable correlation between the degree of seriousness of the fear and the danger. However, it is not all that simple to specify what is meant by a 'reasonable correlation'. There are often large differences between judgements made by risk analysts and laymen concerning different dangers – something we will return to in the next chapter.

It is usually claimed that fear undermines rationality. According to Montaigne 'there is no emotion that can more swiftly bring our powers of judgement out of balance' than fear.[37] Edmund Burke follows this up, asserting that nothing robs consciousness so effectively of all reason as fear.[38] And Heidegger claims that one 'loses one's head' when afraid. He gives the example that people in a burning house often save whatever happens to be close to hand, often something of no consequence whatsoever.[39] Different emotions are closely linked to specific patterns of action, and when an emotion announces itself at full strength, these given patterns of action can overrule all rational considerations; or rather, rationality does not come into the picture, so one does not evaluate the more long-term consequences of the action. Actions that spring quite directly out of emotions can be unlike those we would have chosen if we had carried out a more reasoned decision-making process.

Many such critical descriptions of the role of the emotions – especially fear – in our actions, which take fear to be a threat to rationality, seem to imply that we would be better off with a 'pure' rationality that is not obscured by the influence of the emotions. There are, however, grounds for asserting that an absence of emotions would also lead to irrationality. As mentioned, people with major damage to the amygdala are unable to feel fear, even in life-threatening situations.[40] Such a person will act irrationally because that which is dangerous does not always appear as dangerous, and thus is not dealt with or avoided in a rational way. The absence of emotions deprives us, in other words, of perceptions that are necessary for rational choices of action.

Fear always contains a protention, a future projection, concerning pain, injury or death. Aristotle claims that fear is a certain feeling of discomfort or unrest evoked by the idea of being faced with a destructive or painful misfortune.[41] Hobbes, too, defines fear as the assumption of a future evil.[42] Adam Smith writes that fear does not represent what we are actually feeling at present, but what we may be going to suffer at a later point in time.[43] It is not just something to do with a threatening person or event that ought to be avoided. The core of fear is the assumption of a negative future situation. Although not every negative future situation gives rise to fear, something has to be at stake.

All fear is a fear that something is, has been or is going to be the case. One does not necessarily have to believe that what is feared will actually happen. One can fear something even though one believes that it is *not* going to occur. For example, one can be afraid of being struck by lightning when one hears thunder, even though one at the same time knows that the probability of this happening is infinitesimal. Fear would generally speaking seem to be connected with uncertainty. David Hume emphasises this: "'Tis evident that the very same event, which by its certainty wou'd produce grief or joy, gives always rise to fear or hope, when only probable and uncertain.'[44] Aristotle claims that fear is always connected with hope; that one will only fear if there is some possibility for a way out.[45] Thomas Aquinas is of the same opinion, and therefore points out that those who are damned to eternal perdition will not know fear, since all hope has gone, whereas those who fear always have some small hope of a happy ending.[46] Is it correct that fear implies hope? It does not feel completely convincing. Let us assume that I am trapped in a burning house, far from a fire station and any other form of help, and that there does not seem to be any possible escape. Would I not even so feel a fear of the flames that were constantly getting nearer until they finally surround me, even though I have no real hope of escaping? Now the Aristotelian can claim that even in such a situation I would have a tiny hope of being able to escape the flames, that there can be divine intervention, that the flames will not quite reach me, or that something will materialize and help me. It is difficult, however, to see what sort of evidence the Aristotelian might have for such an assertion – it seems more to have been advanced solely to save the hypothesis that fear implies hope, without there being independent evidence of this. It does not look as if there is a strictly necessary link between fear and hope. On the other hand, it would be unproblematic to claim that fear is *usually* connected with hope. This is, among other things, due to the fact that an absolutely hopeless situation is quite rare – there will nearly always be a possibility, however small it might be, for a situation having a different outcome than that which is feared.

Thomas Aquinas remarks: 'All fear comes from our loving something.'[47] What arouses fear is that which in some way or other threatens one's life-plan. It may a threat to one's life, health, a friendship, a love relationship, social status, etc. One fear can outdo another. The fear of losing face can be stronger than the fear of physical injury, as when as children we challenged each other to carry out ever more death-defying jumps – something that resulted in one's body being covered in bruises. Or soldiers who are afraid of being injured in battle, but who are even more afraid of losing face in front of their fellow-soldiers. From this point of view, 'courageous' acts can in fact derive from fear.[48] Either way, a wish is central to all fear – you can fear x only if you wish for non-x. In this wish one experiences oneself as being placed in a situation over which one does not have full control.

The emotions are the paradigmatic example of an affective dimension in our lives. Another word for emotions is 'passions'. This word derives from the Greek *pathos*, via the Latin *passio*, which means to be suffering. This 'suffering' does not primarily designate pain but passivity, that there is something to which one is exposed, something that happens to one. Aristotle distinguishes between *praxis* and *pathos*, that is, between influencing and being influenced.[49] The emotions are not considered as being self-initiated but as something one, in a sense, receives.[50] One cannot choose an emotion just like that. If one is sad or afraid, one cannot simply choose to have a different emotion that one is more comfortable with. We can influence our emotions in a more indirect way, for example, by placing ourselves in a situation where a certain emotion normally arises. We also possess a certain ability to get rid of an emotion or to suppress it. And we can certainly work on our own emotional life and shape our emotional dispositions. It is clear, however, that our emotions will not necessarily conform to our will.

To experience a given emotion is to experience being in a particular situation to which one has been abandoned. All human perception is conditioned by the situation in which perception takes place, and this situation, quite fundamentally, has an emotional dimension. We can say that the emotion is a condition for something being able to convey meaning in a situation. For an object to be able to appear as frightening, amusing or boring, the situation where the object is encountered must be one with a corresponding emotional potential. To use Heidegger's term, we can say that the fear demonstrates human life's basic *Befindlichkeit*.[51] By this term Heidegger seeks to describe how it is to *find oneself* in this world. To find oneself in the world is to be exposed in the world, to experience the world as a place that contains meaningful and indifferent objects. This 'being in the world' has a basically emotional nature; it is the emotions that enable certain objects to be perceived as meaningful and that, strictly speaking, make participation in the world possible. For Heidegger, we primarily regard objects around us as things to be used, although at times we are notified that these things are 'unusable, contradictory or threatening'.[52] This is only possible because our

41

being-in-the-world is constituted in such a manner that things can affect us in such a way. It is this being-in-the-world that enables anything to be experienced at all as threatening. For Heidegger, emotions are not purely subjective but rather 'the fundamental way in which we are outside ourselves'.[53] At the same time, they put us in contact with ourselves. He writes:

> An emotion is the way we find ourselves in our relation to beings and thus at the same time in our relation to ourselves; the way we are attuned in relation to beings that we are not and to beings that we are. In the emotion the state opens and holds itself open, in which we have dealings with objects, ourselves and human beings. The emotion is itself this open state . . . Here it is important to realise that the emotion has the nature of opening and holding open, and that it therefore can be concealing.[54]

An emotion gives you access to yourself and to the outside world, but precisely because emotions are able to open up these subjects in such a way, they can also conceal, and thus give you an inadequate view of both yourself and the world. Heidegger also seems to be of the opinion that fear is an emotion that will be concealing:

> We become afraid in the face of this or that particular being that threatens us in this or that particular respect. Fear in the face of something is also in each case a fear for something in particular. Because fear possesses this trait of being 'fear in the face of' and 'fear for', he who fears and is afraid is captive to the mood in which he finds himself. Striving to rescue himself from this particular thing, he becomes unsure of everything else and completely 'loses his head'.[55]

In Heidegger's analysis of fear, that which is feared is something that has not yet been realized, something that exists as a menacing possibility that is drawing closer. The feared object 'radiates harmfulness'.[56] The crucial thing is that this harmfulness has not yet been realized, and that there is a possibility that it will not do so. Fear is thus closely associated with uncertainty. This uncertainty can be described as a basic feature of human existence. In fear a fundamental determination of my being is revealed, that is, the fact that I am exposed.[57] At the same time as fear uncovers something about me, it also conceals me from myself. Earlier, I have stressed that fear always contains a projection into the future. Heidegger for his part also stresses the *nowness* of fear – that one is locked in a situation and thereby loses something of one's freedom. He writes: 'The temporality of fear is an expectant, present-making forgetting.'[58] What is forgotten is one's self, or rather, one's own options. The point is that the future, as a field of possibilities, is restricted since one directs one's attention solely at the present threat. One loses oneself since one's attention is concentrated on what is threatening. An emotion such as fear is a way of being present in the world. On the other hand, a world you fear is a place where you can never feel completely at home.

According to Heidegger, one loses sight of one's possibilities in fear. Jean-Paul Sartre, for his part, stresses that 'It is by throwing myself at my own possibilities that I escape fear.'[59] Sartre has an understanding of emotions in general and of fear in particular that differs considerably from that of Heidegger. For Sartre, each emotion has in a certain sense been chosen, and thus it can never eliminate the field of possibilities. Sartre considers emotions as intentional strategies. According to him, emotions are an attempt to change the world via a 'magical transformation' of it. The analysis of fear is a clear example of this, since fear is claimed to be an intentional strategy where the subject attempts to remove –

in a 'magical' way – an object. It ought to be fairly obvious that this magic is not very often successful, as an object seldom disappears simply because one fears it. When this magical strategy fails to work, the subject resorts to flight. Fear, then, is not the cause of flight, as is normally asserted, and flight is not the cause of fear either, as the James-Lange theory proposes – flight is rather a substitution for a fear that does not affect the magical transformation intended by the subject.[60]

Emotions are unreflected, according to Sartre, and by that he means that they take place without being objects of awareness.[61] In fear, awareness is directed towards the object of fear and not towards fear as such. Fear is not self-aware. For that reason, emotions are also something that – despite being the intentional products of the subject – partially elude conscious control. We cannot simply transport ourselves into a particular emotion by wanting to have it. On the contrary, the emotions 'capture' awareness and make it 'passive'.[62] And thus we would appear to be in the same situation as that described by Heidegger above, where fear shuts out one's own possibilities. Sartre, however, seems to believe that the awareness of fear being precisely the own, intentional product of the subject opens up the possibility that one can regain a certain amount of control over it. Because the feeling of fear has been chosen, it can also be deselected in favour of other possibilities. For Sartre believes that we ourselves decide what meaning we are to ascribe everything that surrounds us in existence and how we are to allow it to influence us. In relation to fear, this means that I myself choose to form an ego that fears various things and events. I could, however, have chosen to form a different ego that would have related to my surroundings in a different way.

It can be useful to describe emotions as habits. By that I do not mean to denaturalize the emotions completely, just to stress that our emotional apparatus is malleable. Emotions are not simply something 'given', but something that can be cultivated and changed. Habits can generally speaking be described as acquired responses that people are normally unaware of, but which they can be made aware of. Habits are based on repetition of an ability. Hegel talks about habits as a second nature.[63] This captures something essential about them, since habits are so fundamental and self-evident in our dealings with the world that it would seem that they could not be otherwise. There are physical and mental habits, and tying a tie in a particular way, trying to understand a word in a particular way and reacting emotionally to particular objects and situations can all be described as habits.

Everyone has a host of habits that he or she is unaware of, for the simple reason that consciousness is not normally directed towards them. Habits form more of a 'backdrop' for that which consciousness is directed towards. It is determined by habit *what* we normally look for in a situation of a particular type. Habits select the objects we are to direct our awareness towards, either by our habitually looking at the particular thing or because this thing, for some reason or other, breaks with the habit. Viewed thus, habits are conditions of possibility for perception, but at the same time they narrow down the space of understanding because they will eliminate a certain number of phenomena as irrelevant. A habit expresses a kind of understanding, because it comprises a way of relating to the world.[64] To have a habit is to have acquired a perspective on the world. Habits interact in a complex fashion. Without habits the world would not appear to be meaningful, because habits connect the world together into a whole against which individual things can stand out as meaningful. This also means that the habits we have influence our view of a series of phenomena that are apparently not so closely linked to them.

My hypothesis is that fear is in the process of becoming such a habit. By this I am not so much thinking of strong, overwhelming fear but rather of what could be described as low-intensity fear, although this habitual nature also applies to phobias to a certain extent. The psychologist Isaac Marks, who is one of the world's leading theorists within the field of fear and anxiety disorders, believes that many phobias are to a great extent acquired.[65] The fear behaviour of a mother or father, for example, could be passed on to their children.

It seems that we habitually focus on what is potentially dangerous in everything we encounter in life. We ought to distinguish between fear as a general disposition and fear as an actual emotion. The person who is genuinely afraid of heights is not the person who stands trembling next to you close to the edge of a roof but rather the person who will do anything to avoid every kind of high place. We could say that the latter has so profound a dispositional fear of heights that he or she systematically does everything possible to avoid any situation where fear could manifest itself as an actual emotion. Different situations where we feel fear *feel* different. The feeling of fear is not always the same – it varies not only in intensity but also in quality. The fear of getting mixed up in a fight has a different quality from the fear of falling off a ladder. The distant fear of being infected by an illness that is rampant in a different part of the world is different in nature from the fear of being struck down by a direct physical injury here and now.

In studies of fear, the emotionally intense variant is the type most often emphasized. The type of fear that is predominant in our culture is, as mentioned, more what could be referred to as a low-intensity fear, a fear that surrounds us and forms a backdrop of our experiences and interpretations of the world.[66] It is a fear that has more the nature of a mood than an emotion. The sociologist Zygmunt Bauman writes about what he called a 'diverted fear', a fear that is neither due to being directly confronted with a threatening object nor to one previously having been exposed to such an object. It is rather a fear that manifests itself as a feeling of uncertainty, a feeling that there are possible dangers that may strike without warning and that the world is an insecure place.[67] It is fear as a way of looking at the world, where one's own vulnerability is considered above all.

THREE

Fear and Risk

It's like risk versus reward, baby.
Charlene Shiherlis in *Heat* (1995)

The sociologist Anthony Giddens describes postmodernism as a 'risk culture'.[1] By this he does not mean that human beings today are more exposed to dangers than previously, but that they have a different, and greater, awareness of these dangers. In what Ulrich Beck refers to as the 'risk society' the risk-awareness of citizens is not only based on personal experiences and on second-hand information but also on 'second-hand non-experiences'; risk awareness is not only based on something that has actually happened to someone but also on conceptions of everything that *can* happen.[2] In this risk society, citizens live their lives with the kind of fear described at the end of the previous chapter – fear as a way of looking at the world. A risk society is a culture of fear.

Perhaps the best introduction to what it means to live in a risk society is not to be found in the sociological studies of Giddens or Beck but in Don DeLillo's satirical novel *White Noise* (1985). The novel depicts the life of Jack Gladney, an American Hitler researcher at a small, insignificant college in the Midwest, and his family. The recurring theme is an extreme fear of death, and this fear is fuelled not least by the endless dangers by which the Gladney family feel they are surrounded. The school that the children attend has to be evacuated because of poisonous gas:

> They had to evacuate the grade school on Tuesday. Kids were getting headaches and eye irritations, tasting metal in their mouths. Writhing teachers rolled on the floor and spoke in foreign languages. No one knew what was wrong.

Investigators said it could be the ventilating system, paint or varnish, the foam insulation, the electrical insulation, the cafeteria food, rays emitted by micro-computers, the asbestos fireproofing, the adhesive on shipping containers, the fumes from the chlorinated pool, or perhaps something deeper, finer-grained, more closely woven into the basic state of things.[3]

Everything is uncertain: what is actually dangerous, where the dangers come from and how dangerous they are. Something, though, is obviously dangerous, and there are rumours that one of the people in a protective suit and gas mask collapsed and died while examining the school. Many of the dangers named in the novel are due to chemicals, such as additives in the mother's chewing gum. Modern technology is linked almost unambiguously to risk, not least by numerous references to car and plane accidents. Jack also sees his 14-year-old son lose his hair, and wonders what can have caused this:

Heinrich's hairline is beginning to recede. I wonder about this. Did his mother consume some gene-piercing substance when she was pregnant? Am I at fault somehow? Have I raised him, unwittingly, in the vicinity of a chemical dump site, in the path of air currents that carry industrial wastes capable of producing scalp, glorious sunsets? . . . Man's guilt in history and in the tides of his own blood has been complicated by technology, the daily seeping falsehearted death.[4]

Technology is portrayed as terribly risky because one can never gain a complete overview of its consequences. Heinrich himself is mainly preoccupied by the radiation that surrounds us in our daily lives:

The real issue is the kind of radiation that surrounds us every day. Your radio, your TV, your microwave oven, your power lines just outside the door, your radar speed-trap on the highway . . . Forget spills, fallouts, leakages. It's the things right around you in your own house that'll get you sooner or later.[5]

A basic characteristic of the risk society is that *no one* is out of danger – absolutely everyone can be affected, no matter where he or she lives or his or her social status. This is one of the things that it is most difficult for Jack to accept when a toxic cloud threatens their local community:

These things happen to poor people who live in exposed areas. Society is set up in such a way that it's the poor and the uneducated who suffer the main impact of natural and man-made disasters. People in low-lying areas get the floods, people in shanties get hurricanes and torna-dos. I'm a college professor. Did you ever see a college professor rowing a boat down his own street in one of those floods? We live in a neat and pleasant town near a college with a quaint name. These things don't happen in places like Blacksmith.[6]

But the town *is* hit, and Jack is exposed to the toxic cloud, with uncertain consequences. No one is out of danger. Risk has invaded the lives even of those who previously could feel themselves relatively secure. All this risk awareness leads to the fear of death being the focal point in the lives of Jack and his wife Babette. This fear is so strong that Babette starts to take experimental medicine, Dylar, which is to suppress her fear of death completely. She gets the medicine in exchange for sexual favours given to someone employed at the phar-maceutical company that produces it. And she takes the medicine despite having been told of the risk linked to the use of it: 'I could die. I could live but my brain could die. The left side of my brain could die but the right side could live.'[7] These potential side effects would probably scare off most people from taking such medicine, but Babette's fear is already so strong that she will do anything at all to escape it. In this way, the novel brings out an important feature of a risk society: in our attempts to deal with the risk around us, we often choose means that are worse than the problem they are meant to combat.

The word 'risk' comes from the Italian *risicare*, which means 'to dare'. So risk is connected with making a choice. A risk is something one chooses to take. The question is how much risk we are willing to expose ourselves to, both as individuals and as a society. The answer would seem to be: as little as possible. In present-day discourse, a risk is not something one chooses but rather something one is exposed to against one's will.[8] Today, there are few people who remember that the expression 'risk' could originally have both a negative and a positive meaning, since to take a risk also includes a positive possibility. Today, the concept of risk is almost exclusively negatively charged, with a few exceptions – such as on the stock market and in extreme sport. To a great extent, 'risk' has become synonymous with 'danger'.

There is considerable disagreement about what sort of thing a risk is – if it is something objective or a social construction.[9] There are objective aspects to risk, as there are objective causal relations, but risk is also something more than that. There is also a subjective and social element. A risk does not exist independently of those affected by it. The probability of a given event taking place can in many cases be objectively calculated, but a risk is more than the probability of a given event. A relevant concept for risk must also take into account the role played by the event for the person affected – and this is not an objective relation. Furthermore, it is clear that every relation to a risk is socially situated.

The risk discourse is a process of selection in which one risk is given great emphasis while others are ignored.[10] The reason why certain forms of risk are emphasized at the expense of others is that they fit a larger totality of conceptions, especially of a moral nature, that vary from culture to culture. There is no reason to believe that our conceptions of risk are detached from such social contexts. One aspect that also often applies is that a danger does not capture our attention before someone is found who can be blamed for it. In medieval Europe, the quality of water was so bad that it constituted a serious and constant health risk, but this danger only became a public matter when someone found out that the Jews could be accused of poisoning the water sources.[11]

Every risk is written into a moral discourse. Beck stresses that risk assertions are moral judgements on societal development, even though they pass themselves off as being factual judgements.[12] This element is well developed by the social anthropologist Mary Douglas, who closely links risk to the concept of guilt – more precisely, she explains how the concept of risk is part of a moral and political discourse where guilt is portioned out because someone is being threatened by a danger. To be exposed to a risk is synonymous with being exposed to a moral injustice. It is not the sins of the fathers that haunt their children but rather the risks they have let loose in the world.[13]

The perspective of fear and risk needs victims – without actual or potential victims it loses force. The increase in focus on fear therefore coincides with a corresponding increase in the number of victims. Most people belong to, or have belonged to, a so-called weak group: children, old people, immigrants, women, poor, sick, etc. It is a good idea not to belong to one or more of these groups, for simply by belonging to such a group one is well on the way towards victim status, as an especially exposed individual with a need of protection. To be a victim is to be relieved of responsibility for the situation in which one finds oneself. For victim status to be completely legitimate, another requirement is that the person affected is 'innocent'. The most 'innocent' among us are therefore the best victim candidates – and what is more innocent than a child? The child is therefore portrayed as being subject to an increasing number of dangers. As the media expert David Altheide writes: 'The discourse of fear as a perspective opens up seemingly unlimited terrain for exploring potential victimization of children.'[14] An American study showed that four out of five American children were 'victims of sibling assaults'.[15] Quite ordinary squabbling and fighting among siblings are categorized as 'attacks' that turn children into victims. 'Teasing', which undoubtedly can be annoying for the person exposed to it, no longer seems to exist – instead it has been categorized as 'mobbing' that can harm a child for life.

We make every effort to eliminate all risks from children's lives. Our dread of children being harmed in some way or other leads, it would seem, to our robbing them of important experiences. Of course, one ought to teach children to be careful where there is heavy traffic, and that they should take care with water, electricity, etc. But they should preferably not learn that the world is first and foremost to be met with fear. A development has taken place from considering fear as an emotion children ought to learn to overcome to considering fear as a natural part of their lives.[16] At the beginning of the twentieth century there was a widespread belief that children ought to be brought up not to feel and express fear, since they otherwise would be ill-adapted and neurotic as adults.[17] Today, we seem to have gone to the opposite extreme by impressing on them how dangerous most things on this earth can be. At the same time, we apparently try too hard to protect them against the dangers of this world, symbolized by 'the stranger'. The fear images that are drummed into children are no longer ones of trolls and witches but rather of paedophile assaulters and strangers in general. In the second half of the 1980s and during the '90s there were many media presentations that suggested that all children were in great danger of being exposed to assaults from paedophiles. The problem of the sexual abuse of children should of course never be taken lightly, but instead of a rational assessment of a danger, it was rather paranoia that ruled the day. Discoveries that at the very most could indicate that abuse *could* have taken place were considered as confirmation of the fact that they really had taken place. Many people who had not done anything at all had their lives ruined on the basis of extremely weakly substantiated assertions of assault. In many instances, the accusations were so incredible that warning lights ought to have started flashing – but they clearly did not. The probability of a child being killed by a stranger is so small that it almost ought to be ignored. When children are killed, it is normally someone in the immediate family who is responsible. Occasionally, a child is killed by a stranger, and when that happens it is without a doubt a terrible tragedy, but it is so rare an event that it is hardly a good idea to make that slim possibility the basis of children's relations to all strangers.

Humans have an awareness of risk because our lives are unpredictable and exposed. The problem is that our awareness of risk often produces a systematically distorted picture of the world. We have, for example, a tendency to overvalue causes of death that get a lot of publicity, such as food poisoning and murder. Similarly, we undervalue causes of death that do not get much publicity, such as asthma and diabetes.[18] People most often also believe that more people die of accidents than of illness, even though the opposite is the case. After plane or train accidents, some people avoid travelling by plane or train, taking the car instead because they see train and plane journeys as being dangerous. That is a very unwise choice, because the probability of being involved

54

in a car accident is many times greater. It is estimated that about 1,200 Americans have died after 11 September 2001 because they became afraid of flying and chose to drive their car instead.[19] Not only are people's conceptions of risk often systematically distorted, but at times they are also directly inconsistent, as when one and the same technology, namely radiation technology, is seen as being low-risk in medical use and high-risk in industrial use.[20]

Why do we have such misconceptions about the dangers to which we are exposed? One explanation is that we have a psychological tendency to focus our attention on negative rather than positive events. An important factor is that people have a tendency to regard high-risk information as more reliable than low-risk information, no matter whether it comes from authorities, industry or pressure groups. No matter who communicates the information, people most frequently view the worst scenario as being the most reliable.[21] In addition, people most often have a quite hazy understanding of probability, focusing more on the worst conceivable outcome than on what is most likely. Highly significant statistical differences have little effect on people's conception of risk. No matter how improbable they are, disaster scenarios always create fear.

In general, people get to know about various dangers via the media, and the mass media cultivate 'dramatic' scenarios. News is also entertainment that has to captivate, so attempts are often made to establish a relationship between the viewer and the news being communicated. Ideally, the news item should have a direct relevance to the viewer's own life. Single events are presented within a framework that would seem to represent a social problem, something that can affect 'us all', or at least a large part of the population. This can of course be legitimate in many contexts, but there is a tendency in the actual form of presentation to give every event a greater proportion of drama than there is an objective basis for, since greater proportions are 'better news'. When an accident occurs, for instance, if a mental patient kills a chance passer-by in the street, the tendency in the presentation is to imply that all of us are in danger of being attacked by a fairly large number of such individuals, who ought not to be allowed to wander around freely among the rest of the population.

At any given time, there are a number of dangers that can serve as a subject for press presentations, and it would not be all that difficult to publish a newspaper that exclusively dealt with different dangers. Certain dangers are selected for press coverage and others excluded. However, there is no clear link between the amount of attention given to a phenomenon in the mass media and the danger that it constitutes. Dangers that, statistically speaking, are quite insignificant are often given a great deal of attention, while more serious dangers are neglected. The news value is, in short, not determined by the seriousness of the danger – it is more important for the danger to be 'exciting'. So this danger is centre-stage for a while, until it has been sufficiently milked of follow-up cases, and then it is replaced by a new one.

A recurring feature is for negative news to be considered as better news material than positive, and as a result considerably more room is given to such news in the mass media. A study has dealt with the press coverage of two articles in an issue of *Journal of the American Medical Association*, both of which dealt with the relationship between radiation and cancer. One article discussed a study that showed that white men who had worked at a particular laboratory had an increased risk of leukaemia. The other article demonstrated that there was no increased risk of cancer for people who lived in the vicinity of a nuclear power plant. On the face of it, one might think that the latter, positively angled article got most press coverage, since it was relevant for a far greater number of people than the former, but it was the negative article that got far more coverage.[22]

It is a serious problem that treatment of dangers by the media is so systematically distorted. There is hardly any limit to what is portrayed as constituting a serious health hazard. We have, for example, read newspaper articles that claim that there is an increased risk of thrombosis when one flies long distances, especially if one sits in the cheapest seats, but there is in fact no evidence that this is the case. There are admittedly cases of people who have had a thrombosis on such flights, but it has not been proved that this is due to the strain of the flight. Nor are there enough cases to prove that there is a connection. For all we know, the same individuals could have had a thrombosis even if they had missed the flight and stayed at home.

The illnesses that are given greatest media attention are not necessarily those that claim the most lives. The SARS virus scared the whole world in 2003, but the global death count for SARS is estimated by the WHO to be 774, a figure that has to be considered quite modest. It has been calculated that the SARS panic cost more than US$37 billion globally, and for such a sum one could probably have eradicated tuberculosis, which costs several million people's lives every year. I do not want to belittle the potential danger that SARS represents, but it is problematic that the mass media in particular talked about the virus in terms that tended to maximize the crisis.

From time to time, some virus or other appears on the scene that is very scary because it has an extremely high mortality rate. Examples of this are the Ebola and the Marburg viruses. We ought to recall here, however, that there are very few grounds for believing that this type of virus can ever develop into an epidemic – they often kill their victims so quickly that they quite simply do not have time to infect all that many people. As far as Ebola is concerned, it is worth noting that it was not Ebola at all that claimed most lives when it broke out in the Congo in 1995 but sleeping sickness. Since the Marburg virus was first identified forty years ago, in 1967, six outbreaks have been registered and, according to the WHO, it has claimed a total of 467 lives. Two to three times as many Norwegians die every year of common influenza.[23] Epidemics are relatively rare – that is why they cause such a stir when they occur. Today, epidemics have become almost an everyday affair, as we are constantly being bombarded with information about all potential epidemics – or pandemics for that matter. Pandemics occur once in a while: on average there are two to three influenza pandemics every century. The worst one in the last century was the Spanish Flu, which had a mortality rate of about 3% and cost 50 to 100 million human lives.

Epidemics can be considered as inextricably linked to the growth of civilization, which has made it possible for us to become the type of beings we are – agriculture, urbanization, commerce, etc. – and at the same time has made us more vulnerable to the spread of microbes.[24] And there is no reason to believe that we will ever completely escape their devastation, even though we continue to develop better technology for combating them. With considerable certainty we can state that new epidemics and pandemics will arise, but it is also true that we who live in the richest parts of the world – with good hygiene and good medical treatment facilities – will get by relatively unscathed, while the poor people of the world will suffer a fate that is several times crueller. We ought to fear for their fate, but in our part of the world there is not all that much reason for concern.

The average increase in longevity alone indicates that an increasing number of people are getting through life without succumbing to serious accidents, illness, violent crime, etc. The life-expectation in the UK is 81 for women and 77 for men. Since 1950, the average age globally has increased by almost a fifth. If we look at the developing countries in isolation, the average age expectancy has more than doubled in the course of the twentieth century – from 30 to 65. There are, of course, considerable geographical variations: the average child born in such strongly AIDS-affected countries as Botswana, Mozambique, Rwanda, Zambia and Zimbabwe is expected to die before reaching the age of 43, while a corresponding child in an average industrialized country is expected to reach the age of 78. Nevertheless, it is important to underline that life expectancy is increasing in the vast majority of locations.

Pain, sickness and death are a smaller part of our lives than they were for previous generations. If we fall ill, we have a greater chance of being cured than ever before. It is not all that long ago that a small wound could turn into a life-threatening infection because one did not have antibiotics. Despite this, people did not become panic-stricken. Of course, we continue to fall ill. It is undoubtedly serious to be struck down by cancer, for example, but over half of those who get cancer in the UK survive the illness.[25] The incidence of cancer is admittedly increasing, but this can to a great extent be explained by our living to a greater age – and the risk of cancer increases significantly with age. If a man, for example, has a 20% chance of contracting prostate cancer during his lifetime, this does not need to be all that worrying, precisely because we are talking about a risk spread out over a whole life. Since the risk increases with age, a 40-year-old will have much less than a chance in a thousand of contracting prostate cancer in the near future, and such a low degree of probability ought not to be a problem to live with without worrying too much.

We do not have all that much faith in the system of medical treatment. According to a survey carried out for the pharmaceutical company Pfizer in 2005, 67% of those asked did trust their regular doctor, but only 49% had faith in public hospitals, 36% in private hospitals and 32% in chemists, while pharmaceutical companies could manage only 7%.[26]

No less than 22% of those who had been treated by a doctor during the past five years were not convinced the treatment had been adequate. And 66% were worried that the public health service would not give them good care in their old age, with 51% fearing that they would not get satisfactory medical treatment. Widespread mention in the mass media fuels this mistrust.

A serious example is the hysteria that arose concerning infant vaccines. In 1998 Dr Andrew Wakefield published an article in the recognized medical journal *The Lancet* in which he claimed, among other things, that there was a possible link between infant vaccines and autism.[27] The article was given massive press coverage, especially in the UK and USA. It gradually became clear that Wakefield's claim was untenable. *The Lancet* distanced itself from the article and admitted that it should never have been published. Ten out of the twelve co-authors of Wakefield's study also publicly distanced themselves from Wakefield's interpretation of the research results. Despite the fact that Wakefield's study had been totally discredited, media articles continued to say that this vaccine was dangerous, and this resulted in many parents not having their children vaccinated, something that in turn led to many children falling ill.[28] Fortunately, the vaccination figures have now begun to increase once more.

The same medical technology that cures us also makes us more afraid. Not least, it has made us aware of the fact that we can be ill without experiencing any symptoms at all.[29] In a sense, illnesses have moved from the area of the visible to that of the invisible.[30] We cannot rely on how we experience our own state of health, and we can become patients at any time. This undermining of the spontaneous trust we all have in our bodies, that they will tell us if something is wrong, creates uncertainty and fear. It is probably an important reason why the number of doctor consultations – and of doctors – has increased dramatically over the past decades:

we no longer trust in our own health being satisfactory, even though we do not have any symptoms that could indicate something else. Zygmunt Bauman sums up this situation well:

> Instead of being perceived as a single incident that has a beginning and an ending, illness has begun to be perceived as a permanent companion of health, health's 'other side' and as a constantly present threat: it calls for permanent alertness and must be put down and held at bay day and night, seven days a week. Health care becomes an eternal battle against illness.[31]

Every measure to contain a health hazard contains within it new dangers. We have been told, for example, that we ought not to expose ourselves to too much sunlight, since this increases the risk of skin cancer, but we are then told that too little exposure can lead to a serious vitamin D deficiency, which in turn leads to a weakened immune response – and thus to an increased risk of cancer. So it is not all that easy to find one's way around in the forest of assertions as to what, all in all, exposes us to the most danger. And an ever-increasing amount of medical treatment is now directed against so-called iatrogenic illnesses, that is, illnesses caused by previous medical treatment.[32] From that point of view, it is not surprising that people get worried.

Much fear is connected with food. Food safety is a constant source of media coverage, and if someone really believed all we are told about the dangers connected with food, they would presumably never eat anything again. There is scarcely an item of food that has not been linked to some health hazard or other. Many people are also afraid of becoming ill as a result of pesticide residues in food. It is doubtful whether a single person has died from such pesticides. A number of people die from malnutrition and a few from food poisoning, but the amount of pesticides present in the food we eat is simply too small to cause us any harm. John Krebs, who led the British Food Standards Agency, claims that a normal cup of coffee contains just as large an amount of natural toxins as an average consumer acquires in the way of synthetic toxins from pesticide residues in the course of a year.[33] The conclusion one ought to draw from this is not that the cup of coffee is particularly dangerous but rather that the pesticide residues are so far below the body's limit values as to be harmless. There is quite simply no evidence that the tiny residues of pesticides in food cause any health damage at all, not even in the long term, where one can assume an accumulated effect.[34] In the press, however, we see incredibly small amounts of toxins being presented as a health hazard. No account is taken of the fact that the crucial thing is the *amount* of toxins. One can be frightened by reading that every day the body acquires dioxins, since they are highly toxic and are stored in the body for a long time. In actual fact, we take in dioxins with every bite of food, every mouthful of water and every breath. The crucial thing, however, is that the amount of toxins in emissions and food is so strictly regulated that the everyday doses pose no health threat. In small amounts, many toxins can actually be good for us. Producers of organic food, who probably have good intentions, try to create an impression that food from conventional agriculture is dangerous for us – but there is no basis for this assertion. In the UK, the Soil Association had to withdraw a brochure that claimed that organic food tasted better, was healthier and better for the environment, because the Advertising Standards Authority could not find any convincing evidence for these assertions. The producers of organic food create the impression that non-organic food is dangerous, but there is in fact hardly any scientific basis for claiming that organic food production is to be preferred to conventional food production in terms of our health or the environment.[35]

A widespread misunderstanding is that the 'natural' must of necessity be good for us, while the 'synthetic', 'man-made' or 'technological' is the great danger. Technology has enabled us to restrict many of the dangers to which nature formerly exposed us. When we do not manage to do so, when accidents and natural disasters continue to occur, it is ever increasingly claimed that this must ultimately be explained by referring to humans interfering with nature. But we ought to remember just how many disasters have actually been averted precisely by our interfering with nature. Furthermore, we ought to note that the 'old' dangers generally speaking do greater harm than the 'new' ones. If you want to get through a working life without any serious work-related injury, you will normally do well in choosing a hi-tech occupation rather than a low-tech one. It is several times safer to work at a chemical plant than to be a lumber-jack.[36]

Technology is often portrayed as something alien to humanity. But in actual fact, technology is perhaps the most human thing one can imagine. Without technology we would not be able to exist as the kind of beings we are. Left at the mercy of our own purely animal qualities, we would have succumbed to extinction long ago. It could be said that technology made it possible for man to develop. More polemically, you could say that it was not man that invented technology, but technology that invented man. 'Natural' man – if by that we mean non-technological man – has never existed and never will. The technology our distant forefathers developed – such as a the stone axe – made lib-eration from nature's supremacy possible, which in turn enabled beings such as us to develop. Technology released resources for the development of a larger brain – not least language. So there is something basically wrong about por-traying technology as something non-human – on the con-trary, what is human has always depended on technology in order to be human. Technology permeates every aspect of our lives.

Man has always been one step behind in relation to technology, in the sense that technology has opened up new possibilities for what humans can be. Technology does not consist of aids that allow us to remain unaffected. If anything, it changes our practices – and thus us as well. Technology creates a kind of 'second nature', changing both world-pictures and ways of life. It makes it possible for us to conquer many of the restrictions imposed on us by nature, for example, the fact that we can constantly communicate with each other over vast distances. The problematic element in this connection is that to a great extent we are exchanging one form of dependence for another – we liberate ourselves from nature only to be subject to the supremacy of technology.

We are also always one step behind, in the sense that we can never gain an overview of all the consequences of new technology. Technology develops faster than culture. We have long since passed the stage when we could keep up with technology. We are incurring an ever larger *comprehension lag*. It is difficult for us to acknowledge this fact because it means that we are exposed to an outside world that will always contain the unforeseen. This acknowledgement of the unforeseen cannot be eliminated and it clashes with a basic perception in a risk society: that existence ought to be able to be made the object of complete control. There is no room for the accidental – this is nothing else than an overlooked or wrongly assessed risk. An extreme expression for this way of thinking is the decision by the *British Medical Journal* to forbid the use of the word 'accident' in its columns.[37] The justification of this is that an 'accident' is often understood as being something unforeseeable, but since most injuries and their causes are foreseeable, one ought not to use the expression. This decision led to a great debate in the journal, with not everyone equally impressed by this semantic decision. It is, of course, possible to argue that by 'accident' all that is often meant is an unintentional event. In that case, one could rightly refer to an event as an accident even though it was foreseeable by people other than the one who brought the incident about. It should also be pointed out that there is broad agreement nowadays that it is, generally speaking, impossible to foresee events with 100% certainty, only with a certain degree of probability. Despite this, the important thing in this context is that the *British Medical Journal*'s decision implies that human life in principle is absolutely controllable and that all of us have a kind of obligation to adopt a calculating attitude towards our surroundings.

Our lives, however, are not completely controllable. The Norwegian doctor Ståle Fredriksen adopts an interesting angle on health by making 'bad luck' the central concept.[38] To what extent a person falls ill or not does not simply depend on choices the person himself or his surroundings could or ought to foresee the consequences of, but on luck and bad luck. He draws attention to three kinds of luck: (1) constitutional luck, that is, what sort of genes we are born with, immune response, etc.; (2) circumstantial luck, that is, what sort of situations we encounter; (3) consequential luck, for instance, the unforeseeable consequences of the choices we make. Whether or not a person falls ill depends on all three of these factors, and it is an illusion to believe that everything can be made the object of control. Whether or not one contracts cancer, for example, depends to a very great extent on individual dispositions. Most people who sunbathe a lot do not get skin cancer. Most people who smoke do not get lung cancer – even though it must be pointed out that smoking is a high-risk behaviour that is difficult to match. Our lives will of necessity be connected with uncertainty. The question is what stance we ought to adopt towards this uncertainty.

A risk culture is one where, to a greater extent than ever before, one bases oneself on 'expert assessments', while at the same time being highly sceptical about their reliability. With secularization – what the sociologist Max Weber called the demystification of the world – it was science rather than religion that was to protect us against danger. The problem is that the self-same science also appears to a great extent to constitute the greatest threat. In films, scientists are often portrayed as obsessed individuals who want to put an end to the world as we know it. By watching old films one can often catch a glimpse of what that age feared most, with films from the 1950s often dealing with nuclear experiments that have created terrifying, mutated monsters, while environmental damage and disease dominate the presentation of science in films from the 1970s.[39] Ulrich Beck writes that 'the sources of danger are no longer ignorance but knowledge'.[40] Usually, though, it is precisely a lack of knowledge, the impossibility of knowing all the consequences of a given act or invention, that is emphasized in connection with the issue of risk. The sociologist Niklas Luhmann claims that technological advance is so swift that we do not have enough time to gather necessary information, which in turn leads to our capacity to make rational choices being undermined.[41] One might say that in a high-tech society every decision to act has to be made on an unsound basis.

The philosopher Hans Jonas advocates what he calls a 'heuristics of fear'.[42] He presents this fear as a moral imperative. This is not a fear that degenerates into hopelessness, but rather a fear that also contains a hope that it is within our power to avoid what is feared.[43] The basic characteristic of Jonas's position is that we must give the negative prognoses precedence over the positive ones and base ourselves on the so-called precautionary principle. But Jonas's principle is extremely vaguely formulated, and it is unclear *how* serious a danger has to be for the principle to override usual cost-benefit analyses. At certain points he seems to assume that it mainly has to do with what we can call total catastrophes. He says, for example, that we can live without the highest good, but we cannot live without the highest evil.[44] If in our attempts to make the world a better place we risk at the same time letting 'the greatest evil', a total catastrophe, into the world, we ought not to take such a risk. That would be irresponsible. But there are not many potential catastrophes of such a scope – and the principle will in that case be invoked extremely rarely.

At first glance, the precautionary principle seems like a good idea, since all of us have been brought up with such adages as 'Better safe than sorry'. As an explicit principle it emerged in the 1970s, although there are plenty of earlier examples of this way of thinking.[45] The principle has gained broad recognition, and is included in many countries' national legislation and in international treaties. The precautionary principle is also mentioned in public reports, White Papers and the like – especially in relation to issues to do with health and the environment. The principle is mentioned almost routinely in order to show that one is 'responsible', but typically the content of the expression is not clarified.

The two central aspects of the precautionary principle have to do with uncertainty and harm. Uncertainty can have many dimensions: causal relations, the scope or effect of possible countermeasures, etc. Uncertainty will always exist. Based on a requirement of complete certainty, every act will take place on an unsound basis. The precautionary principle is meant to be an answer to the question of the attitude one ought to adopt towards this uncertainty. What does this principle mean more specifically? It is not all that easy to answer that, since there are more than twenty definitions of it, some of which, into the bargain, contradict each other.

Some of the definitions are so weak that practically no one has any difficulties worth mentioning in accepting them. It is, for example, quite unproblematic to accept that one can implement measures to prevent potential harm, even though one does not have indisputable evidence that something is harmful. There are also many examples of it being reasonable to assume that something is harmful, even though one lacks knowledge of the exact causal relationships. In the strongest versions of the principle, on the other hand, proof is required that something is harmless for it to be allowed – Greenpeace, for example, has advocated forbidding all dumping of waste where it has not been documented that the waste is harmless – and this is a requirement that in practice it is impossible to fulfil. Between these two extremities there are many inter-mediate positions. Some definitions require a potential *catas-trophe*, while others require only a potential *danger to life and health*. Some emphasise economic relations, that there must be 'cost-effective measures', while others do not mention this. Some consider the principle to be a criterion for decision-making, while others do not. There is no agreement as to which definition is the right one, although certain definitions are given more weight than others.[46] Nevertheless, it is prob-lematic when a political measure says only that the underly-ing principle is a precautionary one, without specifying which version of the principle one is thinking of.

Many pressure groups try to get a very strong interpreta-tion of the principle accepted, with every risk being consid-ered unacceptable. The strongest versions of the principle can function as a serious hindrance to inventions that are genuinely favourable for us. In a survey carried out in 2003, a number of scientists were asked which medical, techno-logical or scientific advances would, in their opinion, have been prevented if science had been governed by the precau-tionary principle.[47] The list included antibiotics, aspirin, blood transfusions, cars, chlorine, electricity, light bulbs, organ transplants, the Pill, planes, radar, radio, space travel, trains, vaccines and x-rays. The survey was based on a very strong formulation of the principle, but even so the results indicated that the fundamentally negative orientation of the principle is problematic.

The precautionary principle is not harmless. The more precautionary we are, the more frequently will we introduce measures to prevent harm that would never have materialized. All these measures make a demand on resources that result in less resources being available. If one uses the strictest versions of the principle as one's point of departure, and instead of reserving the principle for catastrophes, broadens it to include all types of instance where there can be negative impact on health or the environment, the economic cost to society is potentially astronomical. On the other hand, if one reserves the principle for potential catastrophes, it will only be used extremely rarely, since there simply are not all that many potential catastrophes.

If a complete risk assessment is to be made, it is not enough just to look at potential harmful effects of introducing a new technology; one must also look at the potential harmful effects of *not* doing so. There is, for example, a risk attached to very thorough testing of medicine that is potentially live-saving, since this may result in patients dying while waiting for the approval of the medicine. If one really is to be precautionary, one ought to take both the advantages and the disadvantages of a given measure into account, but then it would seem that one ends up with a perfectly ordinary cost-benefit analysis.

Many efforts to reduce the amount of danger have actually increased it instead. The problem is that people stare blindly at the damage caused by a given practice without taking the positive effects of the practice into account. Only looking at the potential danger connected with the use of a product can have serious consequences. Responsible risk-thinking must also take the dangers of *not* beginning to use a product into account. An example of this that is often cited is the cholera epidemic in Peru in 1991, where over 700,000 people fell ill and several thousand died because chlorine was removed from sources of water in order to avoid its possible harmful effects.[48] Another, even more extreme example is the pesticide DDT. This is a highly toxic substance that breaks down very slowly. It was discovered as early as 1874, but the capacity of the substance to kill insects was not proved until the mid-twentieth century. Despite the fact that there was no scientific proof that DDT was particularly dangerous for human beings, environmentalists succeeded in getting the substance banned in many countries. The idea was that one had to be 'precautionary' about the threat that DDT might pose. In our part of the world, the ban did not have very great consequences, but many countries and international organizations put pressure on developing countries for its use to be stopped there, too. What was the problem, then, with the great reduction in the use of DDT? It is an inexpensive agent that has proved itself highly effective in combating malaria-carrying mosquitoes.[49] When DDT was used less, the mosquitoes returned, and with them the malaria, leading to the illness and death of many people. It is difficult to estimate the exact future, but the usual figure given is about 50 million people, although there are estimates as high as 90 million. DDT is no miracle cure, and in many areas mosquitoes have developed a resistance to it, so that other solutions have to be sought. Nevertheless, it is clear that the fight against DDT led to a very heavy loss of human life.

As we have also seen, a number of innovations that have benefited us would perhaps not have been initiated if the precautionary principle had been invoked. The same naturally applies to today's inventions and those of tomorrow. Rather than being a principle on which action is routinely based, it would seem that it ought instead to be used to a quite modest extent – and then only in a weak version and when the doubt or uncertainty is well founded. People ought, basically, to be cautious about being precautionary.

In a precautionary world, the future is dominated by dangers rather than possibilities. Future threats become the cause of present changes. We live with a *telos* that is constantly directed towards a catastrophe. If one threat is averted, there is always an infinity of new ones in the offing. There are no limits to the possible extent of the combating of all these dangers. Normally, fear seeks to conserve. Change is perceived as a risk, and thus as something dangerous. For every change can be a change for the worse. The sociologist Frank Furedi calls this the 'conservatism of fear'.[50] This policy opposes change – it wishes to maintain the status quo. If it is to embrace a change, it is a matter of reaching *back* to something more 'original'. This is an important reason why the political landscape began to behave so strangely, with former 'radical' forces appearing to be highly 'conservative', and former 'conservatives' suddenly appearing to be 'radicals'. Furedi writes about the 'radical' movement:

> Yes, they are radicals, but theirs is a radicalism oriented entirely against change. It is the fear of the future and of the consequences of change that shapes the imagination of this movement. The ethos of sustainability, the dogma of the precautionary principle, the idealization of nature, of the 'organic' – all express a misanthropic mistrust of human ambition and experimentation.[51]

This mistrust is particularly directed towards changes that are urged on by capitalism and science. We choose the strategy of minimizing evil rather than of promoting good. In many instances, this is a wise strategy, but it does not mean it ought to be the *only* strategy.

The social scientist François Ewald stresses that risk-thinking has a tendency to grow, to spread more and more and that it creates a policy of prevention.[52] Such a policy attempts to prevent not only actual dangers but also potential ones – and there are endless potential dangers. Ewald writes:

> Risk has acquired a kind of ontological status. Life is
> henceforth marked by an essential precariousness. Death
> is not beyond life. Instead, it is inscribed into life, it
> accompanies life in the form of risk – from the infinitesi-
> mal risk of this or that pollutant to the total risk of catas-
> trophe or the nuclear menace. With one difference: Risk
> does not represent only a virtual threat or something that
> is merely possible, but is entirely real. Risk gives effective-
> quantifiable presence to that which is merely possible.
> This new relation of life to itself and to death can no
> doubt engender anxiety and a kind of collective and indi-
> vidual frenzy of self-protection.[53]

There is no objective yardstick for what an acceptable risk
level is – it is a pragmatic issue. The problem is that there is
no upper limit for how much security can be insisted on,
since further security measures can always be taken. These in
turn will often reduce our freedom and room for action, and
will thus affect our quality of life.

As Ewald emphasizes, the risk perspective does also open
up new possibilities for *living* in the risk. One can use it to
give life a new intensity. Many people voluntarily expose
themselves to situations where, in some sense or other, they
feel fear. In other words, fear can be extremely attractive.

FOUR

The Attraction of Fear

A frightening world
is an interesting world to be in
in the Forbidden City
or on The Roof of the World
or at the receiving end
of the nine o'clock news
However you put your mind to it
you can find fear where you choose

Magazine, 'Because You're Frightened', *The Correct Use of Soap* (1980)

Nietzsche complains that the world has lost much of its charm because we no longer fear it enough.[1] This diagnosis hardly seems to apply to our age. The emergence of the culture of fear can scarcely be said to have made the world more charming, either. There is, however, an interesting point here in Nietzsche, for fear is linked to charm – at least, in the original meaning of the word. 'Charm' comes from the Latin *carmen*, which means 'incantation' and designates an attraction. A world from which all fear has been eliminated would seem to be very unattractive. It is reminiscent of the society Nick Cave describes in the song 'God is in the House' (2001):

Well-meaning little therapists
Goose-stepping twelve-stepping Teetotalitarianists
The tipsy, the reeling and the drop down pissed
We got no time for that stuff here
Zero crime and no fear
We've bred all our kittens white
So you can see them in the night

Fear lends colour to the world. A world without fear would be deadly boring. Biochemically speaking, fear is related to curiosity, something that can be an important reason why exciting films and experiences are so entertaining. Novels, films and TV series designed to fill people with tension and fear are among the most popular. The author Stephen King is said to have sold about 250 million copies of his novels. Such a fascination with the frightening is of course no new phenomenon. We find examples of this in the art and literature of both antiquity and the Middle Ages. It was not, however, until the mid-eighteenth century that the frightful became a central aesthetic category – not least with the emergence of the Gothic novel.[2]

There is without a doubt something delightful about being terrified almost out of one's wits by a novel, film or computer game. You think you have become hardened after having read and seen so many, and that nothing will ever have quite the same effect again, but then something new comes along that takes you to a domain of terror previously unknown to you. Reading tales by Edgar Allan Poe and H. P. Lovecraft was a great strain on my nerves as a child – I thought it was so sinister that I hardly dared read another page, yet I could not stop myself from reading on even so. I can remember when the film *The Silence of the Lambs* (1991) came, and how I sat on tenterhooks on my cinema seat. I was even more petrified when, when far too young, I saw Ridley Scott's *Alien* (1979), where a not insignificant part of my horror came from the artist H. R. Giger's monster being only hinted at for most of the film. At best, computer games can be even more sinister than both novels and films, because you yourself are taking part in the fictional universe in a more direct way, and during games in the *Silent Hill* series, for example, I had hairs standing out on my arms continuously for so many hours that it seemed possible they would stay that way permanently. There are few aesthetic experiences that can rival feeling such terror so profoundly and intensely.

One can wonder what it is about such films and the like that is so attractive, considering the fact that we otherwise tend to shun everything that scares us. As mentioned earlier, the typical response to fear is to try and create the greatest distance between ourselves and what it is that scares us – but here we have sought it of our own free will. Our reason for doing so is that these experiences somehow give us a positive feeling and fulfil an emotional need. To be strongly affected by something gives our lives a kind of presence. And it can be irksome to feel that life is emotionally just ticking over, that one's inner life lacks zest. It is then that emotions that are basically negative can appear to be positive alternatives to this inertia. Warren Zevon captures this well in the song 'Ain't that Pretty at All' (1982):

> I'm going to hurl myself against the wall
> 'Cause I'd rather feel bad than not feel anything at all

But why should we covet a negative emotion when, despite everything, there are a host of positive emotions available? Why should the emotion of fear be so attractive when our emotional register contains so many other emotions that, on the face of it, one would think were many times more attractive? Perhaps part of the answer is that we have a need to experience our *whole* emotional register, and that the fear we experience in forms of fiction, extreme sport and so on breaks with a humdrum 'everydayness'. This might, however, seem to clash with the assertion that we are living in a culture of fear. If we are living in a culture where most things are seen from the perspective of fear, these voluntary fear experiences ought surely to be superfluous. Earlier, though, I emphasized that the fear that primarily surrounds us in this culture is a 'low-intensity fear'. It is not a fear that gives us the great, mind-shaking experiences that set the whole body on alert. It is more a fear that can be described as a constant, weak 'grumbling', yet one that even so results in our protecting ourselves, cocooning ourselves and isolating ourselves from the world around us. In that case, the increasing commonness of boredom can partly be said to be a result of the culture of fear. And a more intense experiencing of fear would seem to be a cure – or at least a partial alleviation – of boredom. The fearful appears to be something *else* and thus something that can counteract a boring everyday life. Boredom forces a move towards what goes beyond.

To see a horror film or play some terrifying computer game are safe ways of experiencing dangers. Oscar Wilde writes about how art expresses reality, that is, life, but in a tamed form, so that we are not injured. That is why art is to be preferred to life:

> Because Art does not hurt us. The tears that we shed at a play are a type of the exquisite sterile emotions that it is the function of Art to awaken. We weep, but we are not wounded. We grieve, but our grief is not bitter . . . It is through Art, and through Art only, that we can realise our perfection; through Art, and through Art only, that we can shield ourselves from the sordid perils of actual existence.[3]

Art, for Wilde, becomes a privileged space where we can experience all the emotions that life can offer us, without having to pay the price that these emotions are often linked to in real life. Violent and frightening fictions can be good media for the processing of our emotions. Children too can benefit from this, so as to learn to master their fear.[4] The reason why we seek out these experiences is, nevertheless, not that we believe they will help us master life but quite simply because they are productive in themselves.

That which rouses an aesthetic reaction, where we take pleasure in something we fear at the same time, is often something evil. Jean Genet introduces his autobiographical *The Thief's Journal* (1949) by writing that he has been driven 'by a love of what we call evil'.[5] He wants to 'seek a new paradise' by 'enforcing a pure vision of evil'.[6] The crucial thing is whether or not an act is beautiful; the ethical is subordinate to the aesthetic.[7] Every act, even treachery, can be beautiful. And every objection that an act is immoral will be completely futile, because an ethical objection will not, as a matter of course, outdo an aesthetical one. Genet writes:

> Moralists with their good will come a cropper against my dishonesty. Even if they are actually able to prove that an act is despicable because of the harm it causes, I am the only one who can decide if it is beautiful or elegant, and I do so solely on the basis of the song it awakens in me; that is what decides whether I will reject or accept it. Therefore no outside person can bring me back onto the right path.[8]

Genet is here influenced by the ideas of, among others, Charles Baudelaire. In a draft of the preface to *Les Fleurs du mal* (1857), Baudelaire notes that he is seeking 'to extract beauty out of evil'.[9] Everything can be made beautiful, but Baudelaire seems mainly to link the beautiful to evil, claiming for example that murder is the most precious of beauty's jewels.[10] Morality is subordinate to aesthetics, and good and evil become, first and foremost, aesthetic categories: 'we can find pleasure in the vilest of things'.[11] In his diaries, Baudelaire writes that 'the most perfect ideal of masculine beauty is *Satan*.'[12]

Prior to Baudelaire, similar thoughts were also discussed by Thomas De Quincey in his essay of 1827, 'Murder Considered as One of the Fine Arts'.[13] The shocking thing about De Quincey's text is that he advocates looking at a murder not from a moral standpoint but rather from an aesthetic perspective, that is, in relation to taste.[14] The fact that 'Murder Considered as One of the Fine Arts' is also satirical does not really make it any less offensive. De Quincey is not starting from scratch here, either, but is developing ideas expressed by Edmund Burke and Immanuel Kant. In his study of the Beautiful and the Sublime, Burke writes that one could announce one's intention to stage the most sublime, gripping tragedy, with the most brilliant of actors, without sparing anything when it came to scenography, and to add the most exquisite music – and then let it be known that a high-ranking criminal was to be executed on the square outside. The result would be that the theatre would be empty in no time, he claims.[15] He is probably right about that. It is conceivable that all these people flocked to the public execution out of a strong moral feeling, and that they quite simply wanted to witness justice being done in full, although this explanation is not particularly convincing. It would be something other than moral considerations that attracted them to the place of execution. Burke points out that we find it satisfying to watch things that not only would we be unable to get ourselves to carry out but would rather not have seen carried out.[16] He points out, in other words, that there is a contradiction between the aesthetic and the moral reactions to certain events. The crucial thing about the above example, however, is the emphasis on sublime reality outdoing sublime art.

Burke points out a source of aesthetic pleasure that is essentially different from the delight of experiencing the beautiful, an enjoyment that was dark, amoral and asocial. He stresses that the strongest emotional experiences we have are linked to the feeling of being threatened. And this feeling is raised to the Sublime.[17] There is, however, a difference between feeling real fear and having a sublime experience. If we believe that life and limb are in real danger, we will be unable to feel any pleasure – it feels quite simply dreadful. A tornado, for example, can be a sublime sight, but only if you are at a distance and not in immediate danger of being sucked up into it. When an element of distance is added, so that we feel more secure, everything changes, and the experience of the Sublime opens up for us. But there must be fear involved, since fear is the basic principle of the Sublime.[18] Burke's fundamental premise is, then, that fear creates pleasure when it does not get too close.[19]

Rainer Maria Rilke's description of the Beautiful at the beginning of the first Duino Elegy is in fact a description of the Sublime:

> For beauty is nothing but
> the beginning of terror, that we are still able to bear,
> and we revere it so, because it calmly disdains
> to destroy us.[20]

In his first piece of writing on the beautiful and the Sublime, there is not all that much that distinguishes Kant from Burke, even though he ascribes the 'fearfully sublime' (*das Schreckhaft-Erhabene*) a less central role than Burke does.[21] Furthermore, he does not see fright as a sufficient cause of sublime feelings. In his *Critique of Judgement*, published 26 years later, the distance between Burke and Kant increases. Let us outline Kant's conception of the Sublime before looking more closely at the differences between his position and that of Burke. The experience of the Sublime is one of almost being crushed. Our powers of imagination break down, and all that remains is an admiration or awesome respect of something *immense*. Kant distinguishes between two forms of sublimity: the mathematical and the dynamic. The mathematically sublime has quite simply to do with what is great in nature, such as mountains, oceans or outer space. These objects are so vast that we are unable to grasp them conceptually. The dynamically sublime, on the other hand, has to do with nature as a violent force that can crush us – a gale, for example. Kant claims that the first shock of the Sublime is turned around, in such a way that we gain an awareness of the elevated in ourselves, namely reason, and that judgement therefore finally experiences a feeling of delight. So we can say that the Sublime is only the origin of an indirect delight, as Kant sees it, since the delight does not derive from the actual experiencing of the violent or the infinite but more from reason's awareness of itself as something that can transcend even that which is given for the senses. Seen thus, it is not, strictly speaking, the object that is sublime, rather the person observing the object.

According to Kant, the Sublime arouses a 'negative desire' in us that both attracts and repels.[22] He sums up the most important characteristics of the Sublime in the following passage:

> Bold, overhanging, and, as it were, threatening rocks, thunderclouds piled up the vault of heaven, borne along with flashes and peals, volcanos in all their violence of destruction, hurricanes leaving desolation in their track, the boundless ocean rising with rebellious force, the high waterfall of some mighty river, and the like, make our power of resistance of trifling moment in comparison with their might. But, provided our own position is secure, their aspect is all the more attractive for its fearfulness; and we readily call these objects sublime, because they raise the forces of the soul above the height of vulgar commonplace, and discover within us a power of resistance of quite another kind, which gives us courage to be able to measure ourselves against the seeming omnipotence of nature.[23]

A crucial difference between Kant and Burke has to do with the role they apportion fear in the experiencing of the Sublime. As we have seen, Burke asserts that one has to be secure but that even so the subject is exposed to an almost overwhelming feeling of dread. He emphasizes that consciousness is so filled by the fearful object that there is no room for any other thought.[24] The subject stands there as a more or less passive recipient of something immense. Kant inserts a far greater distance, and believes that the Sublime does not materialize until this immensity has been overcome by man's own reason. He stresses man's freedom as regards what is immense and threatening. It is this overcoming that creates the feeling of delight, while the first, overwhelming feeling is simply unpleasant. Kant therefore writes that the person who is in a state of fear cannot pass judgement on the Sublime: 'He flees from the sight of an object filling him with dread; and it is impossible to take delight in terror that is seriously entertained.'[25] The fear that is linked to the Sublime is no true fear: 'The *astonishment* amounting almost to terror, the awe and thrill of devout feeling, that takes hold of one . . . is not actual fear. Rather is it an attempt to gain access to it through imagination, for the purpose of feeling the might of this faculty in combining the movement of the mind thereby aroused with its serenity.'[26] We can say that the Sublime only appears when what is frightening has in a sense been brought under control. Delight is not linked to the experience of danger, rather to a 'deliverance from a danger'.[27] So we are dealing with a completely different degree of distance in Kant from that in Burke.

De Quincey takes Burke's and Kant's reflections one step further. If the violent in nature can be a source of aesthetic experience – why should not human violence – which perhaps is even more terrifying – also be a source of aesthetic experience? Violence has its own power of attraction. It can be claimed that violence is repulsive, but we can just as easily claim that violence is sublime. There is nothing that prevents either of these judgements from being legitimate. In both cases we are dealing with judgements of taste – and aesthetic taste does not necessarily conform to our moral judgements. This does not mean that moral considerations are necessarily irrelevant in relation to the aesthetic assessment of an object or an event, but they are not necessarily relevant, either.

It is difficult to imagine any human act that distinguishes itself as sublime more than murder, precisely because of its excessive and dread-inspiring nature. Burke's example of the public execution shows that he was open to this possibility, even though he did not develop it. Kant, on the other hand, took the Sublime in a different direction. He admittedly highlights war as something sublime, but it is tamed, controlled warfare: 'war itself, provided it is conducted with order and a sacred respect for the rights of civilians, has something sublime about it.'[28] This can be questioned. Can then a war that is conducted without respect for individual rights not be considered as *more* sublime? Let us take a remark by an American soldier in Vietnam, who talks about the thoughts that struck him when he was standing looking at the bodies of North Vietnamese soldiers:

> That was another of the times I stood on the edge of my own humanity, looked into a pit and loved what I saw there. I had surrendered to an aesthetic that was divorced from that crucial quality of empathy that lets us to feel the sufferings of others. And I saw a terrible beauty there. War is not simply the spirit of ugliness . . . it is also an affair of great and seductive beauty.[29]

Kant would not recognize this as sublime, but rather relegate it to the category of 'the monstrous'.[30] Burke, though, would claim without hesitation that this American soldier was having a sublime experience. Broadly speaking, Kant restricted the experience of the Sublime to encounters with nature, even though he also included certain man-made phenomena, such as the Pyramids, St Peter's in Rome and war. Possibly as an ironic comment on Kant, an enormous toxic cloud is a sublime phenomenon in Don DeLillo's novel *White Noise*:

> The enormous black mass move like some death ship in a Norse legend, escorted across the night by armored creatures with spiral wings. We weren't sure how to react. It was a terrible thing to see, so close, so low, packed with chlorides, benzines, phenols, hydrocarbons, or whatever the precise toxic content. But it was also spectacular, part of the grandness of a sweeping event, like the vivid scene in the switching yard or the people trudging across the snowy overpass with children, food, belonging, a tragic army of the dispossessed. Our fear was accompanied by a sense of awe that bordered on the religious. It is surely possible to be awed by the thing that threatens your life, to see it as a cosmic force, so much larger than yourself, more powerful, created by elemental and willful rhythms. This was a death made in the laboratory, defined and measurable, but we thought of it at the time it in a simple and primitive way, as some seasonal perversity of the earth like a flood or tornado, something not subject to control. Our helplessness did not seem compatible with the idea of a man-made event.[31]

Kant would also probably have consigned this toxic cloud to the category of 'the monstrous', on a par with murder. Nietzsche's mention of pleasure and the Sublime at a world perishing would have been completely alien to him.[32] Kant thus debars himself from examining the seam uncovered by

Burke and that De Quincey took to its extreme by showing human destructiveness to be a source of aesthetic delight.

De Quincey allows aesthetics to outdo ethics by letting the Sublime outdo the beautiful. Crimes are fascinating. Adam and Eve disobey God's command by eating from the Tree of Knowledge, and their sons, Cain and Abel, become the first murderer and the first victim respectively.

Accounts of various types of crime are as old as literature itself, and they often took their motifs from real figures. Well-known examples of this are John Gay's *The Beggar's Opera* (1728), Stendhal's *Le Rouge et le noir* (1830) and several of Dostoevsky's novels. Even so, it must be stressed that all of these were fictionalized presentations. Michel Foucault remarks that a new kind of crime literature had sprung up at the time of De Quincey:

> A literature in which crime is extolled because it belongs to the fine arts, because it can only be the work of people who are exceptions, because it shows what monsters the strong and mighty are, because being a scoundrel is despite everything a kind of nobility. From the shocker novel to Quincey, or from Château d'Otrante to Baudelaire a complete revision of the ethical norms of crime literature takes place – the claim is actually also made that great people have the right to commit crimes, yes, that really great people are exclusively entitled to commit them. Beautiful murders are not something for people who commit crimes for profit.[33]

An aestheticizing of crime in general had taken place. Already in John Gay's *The Beggar's Opera*, later refashioned by Brecht into his *Dreigroschenoper*, ('The Threepenny Opera') Peachum says: 'Murder is as fashionable a Crime as a Person can be guilty of.'[34] This aestheticizing, however, remained within the realm of fiction. De Quincey takes everything one step further. What is radical about him is that he considers reality as art and elevates the most extreme of human acts, murder, to supreme art. The work of art is not, then, the narrating of the murder, but the murder *itself*. The artist is not the author who depicts the murder, but the actual murderer. Here, De Quincey went far beyond, for example, Friedrich von Schiller, who wrote that murder was aesthetically higher than theft, since Schiller was mainly operating within a fictional horizon.[35] There is nothing to indicate that Schiller would consider a real murder as a work of art.

Why did De Quincey consider murder a work of art and the murderer as an artist? Because murder creates an aesthetic response in the observer, and everything that arouses such a response is, as De Quincey saw it, by definition, art – and someone who creates art is an artist. As Burke had already shown in the example of the public execution, reality is greater than fiction and the real murder creates a stronger aesthetic response than the fictional one. Therefore, the murderer becomes the supreme artist. What De Quincey delights in about murder is not the suffering of the victim but the sight of an artist who uses somebody else's body as raw material to create his work. This also means that the perspective from which the murder is considered cannot be that of the victim but has to be the murderer's own – or that of an observer. The distance is thereby created that is required for the experiencing of the Sublime. If one really had to manage to assume the stance of the victim, the fear would be so overwhelming that the aesthetic experience would be impossible. In can be objected here that De Quincey inserted too great a distance, and that the absence of identification with the victim deprives the observer of the fear that is crucial for a sublime experience.

The composer Karl-Heinz Stockhausen fitted in with the tradition from Burke to De Quincey when he stated that the terror attack on the World Trade Center was the greatest work of art ever. Burke doubtless would have considered the attack on the Twin Towers to be Sublime,[36] as would De Quincey. Kant, on the other hand, would have banished this event from the realm of the Sublime. While for Kant it was vital to maintain a connection between ethics and aesthetics, the good and the beautiful, we find a stronger separation of aesthetics from ethics in De Quincey. He writes that we must put morality behind us and consider murder purely from an aesthetical perspective.[37] The separation is not complete, however. De Quincey emphasized, for example, that the murder victim ought to be a 'good person', preferably with a family as well, since the aesthetic quality is inversely proportional to the moral one.[38] An aesthetics of transgression always presupposes morality, since it is morality that makes the actual transgression possible. In short, without morality the aesthetics of transgression has no object. The aesthetic consideration of the crime is not independent of the moral perspective – it presupposes it. The fact that a given act exceeds a moral or legal norm is an important precondition of its aesthetic quality.

Violence can give rise to aesthetic delight, even though we find it morally deplorable. Conflicts of values in modern societies are enacted not only between different social groups – we are perhaps talking just as much about conflicts within the individual subjects taking part in different spheres of values, as for example a moral and an aesthetic sphere. Just as the conflicts between the different groups can be resolved by referring them to a neutral, so can higher authority conflicts within the individual subjects.

Rather than relegate horror films and scary computer games to the bottom shelf of aesthetics – as is not uncommon – I would claim that these are the strongest representatives of the Sublime in present-day art. Of course, most of what is produced within these genres is appallingly bad, but so is most of what is produced within any genre, and the best that is produced within these genres is in no way inferior to the best within any other genre. These genres can be said to have taken Walter Benjamin at his word when he claimed that art in modern times had to liberate the experience via *shock*.[39]

We can be attracted by what repels us. This is an old, well-known point. Hegel's pupil, Karl Rosenkranz, is often credited with the discovery of 'the aesthetics of the ugly', and he was certainly the first person to develop such an aesthetics systematically.[40] It must, however, be pointed out that Burke explicitly wrote that the ugly was fully compatible with an idea of the Sublime.[41] And as early a philosopher as Aristotle made it a central aspect of his aesthetics: 'objects which in themselves we view with pain, we delight to contemplate when reproduced with minute fidelity: such as the forms of the most ignoble animals and of dead bodies.'[42] Here it is the actual imitation, *mimesis*, that in itself is a source of a feeling of delight. Another central concept in Aristotle's aesthetics is *catharsis*, which is normally translated as 'purgation' or 'purification'. Aristotle wrote that tragedy 'through pity and fear effects the proper purgation of these emotions'.[43] Just how Aristotelian *catharsis* is to be understood is a much discussed issue. There is broad agreement that the purgation described takes place in the observer and not in the person depicted in the tragedy; also that Aristotle here connected this with the medical idea of removing something harmful from the human organism. There is, however, some disagreement as to the extent to which Aristotle was also seeking to connect this with older ideas of a religious nature, where certain objects or persons had to be purified after having been exposed to, or after having carried out, actions that contravened certain taboos. The most important thing for our purpose here is that Aristotle says that there is a favourable effect on the observer because he or she witnesses fearful impressions from a scene. What this effect consists of is not evident. It is possible to interpret Aristotle in such a way that we can say that we are dealing with a kind of emotional discharge in which the observer gets rid of inner tensions that it would otherwise be difficult to find expression for in society, and that ought to find such expression there too. Another interpretation is that we are dealing with a processing of emotions in a wider sense. If we read Aristotle's poetics in conjunction with his ethics, *catharsis* can be interpreted more along the lines of contributing to our personal moral development, the aim of which is for the emotions and reasons to be attuned to each other. Aristotle emphasizes that moral teaching has to a great extent to do with learning to feel the right thing in the right way at the right time.[44] We must learn to handle our emotions in such a way that they will enable us to make correct assumptions about situations and will move us to act in accordance with this knowledge. In relation to fear, an important feature of *catharsis* would be to teach us to fear the right things in the right way at the right time. The textual basis of the *Poetica* is so slender that is it difficult to understand exactly what Aristotle includes in this concept, but it is at least uncontroversial that he places great value on the aesthetic experiencing of fear. De Quincey also later links up with Aristotle when he writes: 'For the final purpose of murder, considered as a fine art, is precisely the same as that of tragedy, in Aristotle's account of it, viz., "to cleanse the heart by means of pity and terror".'[45]

It is paradoxical that we actually can take delight in dwelling on objects that arouse the feeling of fear we would normally seek to avoid.[46] We experience what could be called a fear by proxy, where another person – fictive or real – is in a terrifying situation, and we participate in this fear from a distance. In other words, we get the opportunity to experience extreme situations without ourselves being in any real danger. We thereby gain access to sides of our emotional life that are not normally part of our everyday lives. One assumes two roles at the same time: in a sense, one is present in the narrative, film or computer game, but one also stands on the outside and can at any time remove oneself from the situation by closing a book or switching off the TV. In other words, we have control over the situation.

Many people, however, also like to place themselves in a situation where the dangers are real – although in relatively controlled forms. In other words, we leave the perspective of an observer and assume that of a participator. An example of this is so-called extreme sport. Now all forms of sport are connected with an element of risk, but extreme sport differs from other sports since the danger linked to pursuing such a sport is an important part of its attraction. It looks perhaps as if the satisfaction gained from the activity is proportional to the degree of danger. The danger of not only injuring oneself but of actually dying gives one a new awareness of life. At the same time, it is important that the person involved does not feel completely at the mercy of the circumstances, but feels himself to be in control of the situation. The sociologist and anthropologist David Le Breton claims that such a person undertakes a more or less controlled journey into death's domain and brings a trophy back home that is not an object but an experience of living life to the full.[47] Without the element of danger, the experience would simply not provide the same satisfaction. The physical exposure is crucial.

I cannot see any reason for not including such activities in the aesthetics of the Sublime. As Maurice Merleau-Ponty has shown, our whole physicality is a condition for any aesthetic experience, also when we consider paintings and the like.[48] The body is more strongly involved in extreme sport activities, however. While aesthetics has traditionally concentrated on the sense of sight, Burke is an important exception in that he strongly involves physicality in his account of the Sublime.[49] Burke also closely connects the Sublime with the thought of self-preservation, and so it is clear that for him the aesthetic experience does not presume the lack of interest that is central to so much modern aesthetics, especially in Kant. On the contrary, the experiencing of the Sublime will be inextricably linked to the interest in self-preservation. From such a perspective, it is not at all a wish to die that drives the person who indulges in high-risk activities but, on the contrary, a wish *not to die*. In other words, extreme sport testifies to an optimistic conception of reality. The interest in a continued existence is what gives the experience its intensity. The reason for seeking this type of activity is that the fear contained in it gives one a renewed feeling of being present in one's own life.

This can also apply to situations one has not chosen oneself, as is well exemplified in the novel (1996) and the film (1999) *Fight Club*: Raymond K. K. Hessel, who works in a kiosk, who has dropped his studies and seems to have abandoned any ambition to make something of his life, has a pistol put against his head and is told he only has a few seconds left to live. The whole thing is an attempt by the main character Tyler Durden to carry out what could be called an existential pedagogy in which the fear of death is to give Hessel a new, more authentic perspective on his life. After having removed the pistol from Hessel's head and gone away, Durden thinks: 'Raymond K. K. Hessel, your dinner is going to taste better than any other meal you've ever eaten, and tomorrow will be the most beautiful day of your entire life.'[50] The narrator of the novel is also exposed to the same pedagogy, when after a hazardous car drive and an ensuing collision he is told: 'You had a near-life experience.'[51] Along with John Locke we can say that fear gives our lives a shove – without it we would sink into passivity.[52]

It is difficult to imagine that a world completely without fear would be particularly interesting. In an otherwise secure world, fear can break the boredom. A feeling of fear can have an uplifting effect. As the religious historian Jean Delumeau states in his comprehensive study of fear and sin in Western culture from the thirteenth century to the eighteenth, fear has both a destructive and a constructive aspect: it can break you down or open up a new, better relationship to the world.[53]

FIVE

Fear and Trust

Who put this thing together? Me, that's who! Who do I trust? Me!
Tony Montana in *Scarface* (1983)

Fear normally leads to seeking to establish a distance between oneself and that which is feared. A fear culture can therefore undermine the trust many philosophers, theologians and sociologists consider to be one of the most basic characteristics of human relationships.

In *The Ethical Demand* (1956) the Danish philosopher and theologian K. E. Løgstrup suggests that

> We normally meet each other with a natural, mutual trust. This also applies when we meet a perfect stranger. A person must first behave in a suspicious way before we mistrust that person. In advance, we believe in each other's words; in advance we trust each other. This is perhaps rather strange, but it is all part and parcel of being a human being. It would be hostile to life to behave otherwise. We could quite simply not exist, our lives would wither away, would become crippled, if we met each other in advance with mistrust, believed the other person stole and lied, pretended and tried to deceive us . . . But displaying trust involves self-surrender.[1]

Løgstrup considers trust a fundamental characteristic of being a human being, something we cannot live without. As such, trust is not something we decide to have but something that has already been given prior to any decision regarding gain or loss. Special circumstances must arise for it to be replaced by mistrust. Mistrust would not make any sense without a massive background of trust.

Every day we rely on other people in practically every situation we are involved in – that they do not serve us poisoned food, that they tell us the truth, that they do not try to swindle us, and so on. It may be that this trust is abused, but that is the exception rather than the rule. Without trust you would not be able to do anything at all. Imagine a day where you have to calculate all the risks that might come your way, and make sure of the outcome in advance. You would hardly make it out of the front door in the morning. A lack of trust has the obvious consequence that behaviour that presupposes trust will not take place.

The paradigmatic example of trust is that between two persons, though we can also trust animals, groups, social institutions and so on. It is possible to note an increasing mistrust of a number of institutions that previously enjoyed great trust, such as science and the health service. Practically every day, opinion polls are published about a loss of trust in some profession, organization, social institution and the like. Just as striking, however, is the strong increase in various types of security measures, such as alarms and security locks in the home, identity cards and passwords at the workplace, surveillance cameras in public spaces and various control routines in industry and public services.

Towns, which were originally built to protect the inhabitants from dangers from without, have themselves now become more of a source of fear than security. The cityscape is becoming increasingly shaped by various security measures, and in the course of an ordinary day you come into contact with guards, admission cards, door telephones, protective fencing and so on. The wall that is to protect one against what threatens 'out there' has even moved inside the walls of the home, so an industry now exists to protect us there too, by installing alarms, security locks and the like, to prevent intruders from coming in. Security equipment and services presuppose frightened consumers. Therefore there are also considerable economic interests involved in keeping fear in a population at a high level – and preferably constantly increasing that level. Consumers pay for these services in order to be more secure, although it does not actually seem as though they become so. It is difficult to decide what is cause and what is effect here – whether the insecurity leads to all the security measures, or vice versa. It is most likely that they have an intensifying effect on each other. No matter which, it does not seem on the whole that increased investments in security give people an increased feeling of security. The home alarm system and the security locks confirm the image of a dangerous world. There is a constant search for more security, with standards always on the rise. The finishing line never gets any closer, and the gap between the finishing line and the actual security level becomes in itself a source of insecurity. Fear and the striving for even more effective security create an increasingly vicious circle.

The surveillance of citizens has become both more intensive and extensive than ever before. Ever greater portions of our lives have become visible to invisible monitoring systems. The UK has 4.2 million CCTV cameras,[2] one for every fourteen people. Many people are quite simply extremely willing to surrender much of the protection of their private lives in order to protect themselves and society.

All these security measures only make sense against a background of a general mistrust of the people around you. Trusting in your fellow human beings means that you feel secure when you are with them. When trust diminishes in a society, this results in greater social disintegration, with isolated and apprehensive individuals. Everyone is a potential danger to everyone else. Ulrich Beck has formulated it in this way: 'Within the horizon of risk, there is not simply either good nor evil, but rather individuals who are more or less risky. Everyone represents a lesser or greater risk to everyone else.'[3]

The number of books where the explicit or implicit 'moral' is that trusting other people is terribly risky has steadily increased. One example is that of the security expert Gavin de Becker, whose book *The Gift of Fear* (1997) has topped the sales charts in the USA.[4] On the cover it states that 'this book can save your life', and it intends to do so by showing you how to react to all the potentially dangerous individuals who surround each and every one of us in our daily lives. It deals in turn with violence at the workplace, in the home and when on dates. Not least, it focuses on how exposed children are. Admittedly, Becker stresses that we often fear the wrong things, but the main message of the book, even so, is that violence can strike any one of us at any time if we are not on our guard. There is much we ought to on our guard against, according to this book. Charm, for example, is very suspect: 'Charm is almost always a directed instrument that . . . has motive. To charm someone is to compel, to control by allure or attraction.'[5] One should also be highly sceptical of anyone uninvitedly offering to help with anything, since that person is sure to want something from you that you are not necessarily interested in parting with: 'Remember, the nicest guy, the guy with no self-serving agenda, the one who wants nothing from you, won't approach you at all.'[6] The rule that innumerable parents have inculcated in their children – 'Don't talk to strangers' – has also become a maxim for adults. It is hardly an exaggeration to refer to such a book as a study in systematic paranoia.

This mistrust is a recurring feature in much of the self-help literature about relationships. People one engages in an intimate relationship with are almost to be considered as constant threats to mental health – especially that of women. The titles of books by a writer such as Harriet Barkier speak for themselves: *Lethal Lovers and Poisonous People: How to Protect Your Health from Relationships That*

Make You Sick (1992) and *The Disease to Please: Curing the People-pleasing Syndrome* (2001). We also have Susan Forward's *Men Who Hate Women and the Women Who Love Them: When Loving Hurts and You Don't Know Why* (1986) and *Obsessive Love: When It Hurts Too Much to Let Go* (1991), not to forget Albert J. Bernstein's *Emotional Vampires: Dealing with People Who Drain You Dry* (2001). One of the classic contributors to the genre is Robin Norwood, with titles such as *Women Who Love Too Much* (1985), *Letters from Women Who Love Too Much* (1988) and *Daily Meditations for Women Who Love Too Much* (1997). A recurring theme in these books is the danger of ending up being dependent on another person.[7] Many of the characteristics most of us would connect to a normal state of being in love become indications of something pathological, for instance, that you spend an awful lot of your time thinking about the other person or feel utterly crushed when the relationship is over. The underlying 'moral' is 'Be careful!'. People you establish close relationships with can hurt you where it hurts most, resulting in your becoming an emotional cripple. After having read a handful of these books, most people ought to be more or less permanently 'immunized' against the desire to strike up any relationship whatsoever.

Trust is, of course, not necessarily something good – in certain situations trust can be most unwise. On the other hand, there are few things less wise than to go through life with a consistent mistrust of everything and everyone. The sociologist and philosopher Francis Fukuyama describes trust as a kind of 'social capital'.[8] He points out that societies and organizations that are characterized by strong internal trust have much greater success both economically and socially than those with low internal trust. Trust becomes more important the more complex a situation, organization or society is. Trust can function as a tool for handling unpredictability.[9] Apart from the socially integrative dimension, it can be said that trust is a functional alternative to risk calculating and the like. To act on the basis of trust is to act as if a given rationally predictable future will come about, but without having carried out predictions on a completely rational basis. It can, however, prove most rational to choose this less 'rational' procedure, because making reliable risk calculations can be a highly resource-demanding activity. People who trust each other can interact with fewer hindrances than those to be found in a climate of mistrust, where a considerable apparatus of formal regulations and contracts has to be in place. To quote Fukuyama, we can say that mistrust increases human 'transaction costs'.[10] Certain things cannot be predicted, either, so the basic choice is between trust and mistrust – or paralysis of action. Trust makes human transaction possible in situations where a lack of reliable predictions would otherwise result in paralysis of action.

Løgstrup considers trust as being precisely an original phenomenon one cannot go behind for some more profound basis, and he writes: 'Trust does not therefore have to be motivated or justified, as mistrust has to be.'[11] I do not wholly agree. In a fear culture where trust seems to be strongly on the decrease, trust, as far as one can judge, seems to need a motivation and a justification. Such a justification could come from referring to a paradox about trust: one has a reason to display trust to a person, even though that person has not done anything that indicates one ought to display trust to him or her. The reason for this is that a person who is shown trust will willingly do his or her utmost to merit that trust. In a behavioural-psychological experiment at the university in Zurich where students were to allow anonymous fellow students to invest a given sum for them, and the students could choose between a transaction model where a lack of repayment was explicitly connected with punishment, a model where this was only implicit and a model where punishment was nowhere in the picture, it transpired that the group that chose the most trusting model – where punishment was not even a factor – got most money back of the three alternatives.[12] Both trust and mistrust have a tendency to be self-fulfilling prophecies.

Mistrust gives rise to more mistrust partly because it isolates one from situations where a reflected mistrust is learned as a form of social intelligence. We often fear the *unfamiliar* more than the known. That can in itself be an indication that most things are basically not particularly dangerous once we become familiar with them. It has been demonstrated that we are more afraid of people of another 'race' than our own.[13] Since fear has the function that we normally avoid what we fear, we will also have a tendency to avoid people of another skin colour, for instance, and thereby have less chance to learn that they are not actually dangerous.[14] Fear prevents precisely that which could cause it to diminish: human contact. Fear and mistrust become self-perpetuating.

Social fear undermines spontaneity as regards other people, and as such undermines social relations. A fear culture is, then, a culture where trust disintegrates. In a world that is increasingly perceived as dangerous, it is difficult to have trust – you want assurances instead. To explain what trust is, it might be a good idea to start with what it is not. An American philosopher gave a lecture on trust to top management in one of the USA's largest companies in which he underlined the necessity of having trust in one's employees. When the lecture was over, the first question he got was: 'But how can we control the employees?'[15] The question betrayed an attitude that is irreconcilable with trust. A person who has to be subjected to control is precisely a person with whom one cannot have a relationship of trust.

A viable society presupposes that there is a community in which all participants perceive themselves as having a moral obligation towards each other and in which they rely on each other.[16] So Georg Simmel describes trust as 'one of the most important synthesizing forces in society'.[17] For the individual, the function of trust is the same as a hypothesis that is sufficiently tenable to serve as a basis for action. According to Simmel, trust contains an element of 'mystical' belief. He finds it difficult to give a closer definition of this element, describing it, among other things, as an 'in-between state between knowledge and non-knowledge'.[18] In trust there lies an expectation as to how another player is going to act, but there is a leap to this expectation from the basis we have for it. According to Simmel, trust cannot be understood as something absolute – it will always be grad-able, that is, one will always have a certain *degree* of trust towards someone.[19]

In his notes from prison written before being executed for participation in an attempt to assassinate Adolf Hitler, the theologian Dietrich Bonhoeffer explained that:

Hardly any of us have avoided being betrayed. The figure of Judas, who was so incomprehensible to us, is scarcely a stranger any more. The air we breathe is so contami-nated with mistrust that we are close to succumbing. But when we broke through the atmosphere of mistrust, we experienced a trust that we previously had thought impossible. We learnt that if we had trust, we could place our entire life in another person's hands; we learnt boundless trust, towards all the ambiguities our actions were surrounded by. We now know that it is only in such a trust – which will always be a gamble, but to which one gladly says yes – that one can really live and work. We know that one of the most despicable things that exists is to sow and spread mistrust, and that instead one must strengthen and promote trust wherever at all possible. For us, trust will always be one of the greatest, most rare

and happiest gifts in shared human existence, and it arises so fully only against a dark background of necessary
mistrust. We have learnt under no circumstances to surrender ourselves to a scoundrel, but do so unreservedly to
the person worthy of our trust.[20]

Bonhoeffer realizes that trust always involves a 'leap', or an
act of faith if you like. What he advocates, however, is a
reflected trust that always has a background of mistrust.
Trust, then, is always linked to a risk, whether this risk is perceived or not. There are various forms of trust, and they can
be separated from each other according to how they relate to
this risk.[21] The first form of trust is what we can call naive
trust – it is the trust we are all born with. Without such trust,
to our parents and others, we would never be able to grow
up. But this is precisely the trust of a child. As we grow up,
we learn that this trust can be let down. We learn that trust
can be risky. What I call foolish trust is a form of trust
where, against one's better knowledge, one ignores this risk.
An example of this trust is the totally uncritical attitude
members of a sect can have towards their leaders. The trust
that ought to be cultivated, on the other hand, is reflected
trust, which is always linked to the awareness of a risk, which
always contains a trace of mistrust. Reflected trust is always
limited and conditional. Reflected trust is possible only
when the person who shows trust is willing to accept that
there is a certain risk or exposure. When we show trust, what
we assume is that this exposure or vulnerability will not be
exploited.

As Simmel emphasises, trust always contains an extra-
rational element that he compares with mystical belief. It
seems reasonable to assume that this extra-rational element
is, to a great extent, emotionally based. Trust is, to a crucial
degree, linked to one's feelings towards a particular person,
object, society – or the world as a whole. We can also say that

trust is an expression of an optimistic view of reality, since only an optimist will have the belief in his or her fellow human beings that trust expresses. The trusting individual chooses to ignore certain negative scenarios – or at least assume that they will not take place. In today's climate, however, the tendency is the opposite, to ignore the positive scenarios and to base oneself on the negative ones. In a climate of mistrust one is also less amenable to information that could indicate that a phenomenon is not as dangerous as one fears.[22] Viewed thus, mistrust can easily become cumulative. We can say that mistrust becomes part of the habitual fear described in chapter Two. So it is also clear that trust is badly off in a fear culture. Fear has an undermining effect on trust, and when trust diminishes, the scope of fear increases. An increase in fear will also be the result of, and a cause of, a loss of trust.

A fear culture is no trust culture – and that has major consequences on how people relate to each other. Trust can be described as a 'social glue' that keeps human beings together. A society can, however, also be held together by fear, as we will see in the next chapter, but that is a considerably less attractive model.

SIX

The Politics of Fear

Fear. It's the oldest tool of power.

Fox Mulder in *X-Files* (1993)

Cartman: 'I use fear to manipulate people to do my bidding.'
Bart Simpson: 'Uh, isn't that like terrorism?'
Cartman: 'Dude, it's not like terrorism! It is terrorism!'

South Park (2006)

Fear can be considered the basis of all human civilization; it has spurred on the development of everything with which people surround themselves, such as houses and towns, tools and weapons, laws and social institutions, art and religion.[1] In *Scienza nuova* (1744), Giambattista Vico advances such a hypothesis of how all human civilization has its origins in fear.[2] He has it begin with a fear of thunder. It is important that what causes fear is not other individuals but rather something all individuals are exposed to in the same way. When everyone flees from thunder in fear, they are capable of realizing that they all fear the same thing, which gives rise to a common point of reference that can serve as the starting point for a community.

A different model can be found in Niccolò Machiavelli and Thomas Hobbes. While fear is stressed by Vico as being a *common* fear, it is *mutual* fear that is predominant in Machiavelli and Hobbes; individuals fear each other rather than an external threat. The fear that individuals feel of each other, however, becomes a resource for establishing a social community. Both philosophers agree that whoever controls fear in a society is well on the way to controlling the entire society. In both of them, it is a fear of violence that forms the basis for human solidarity. The starting point for all societies that managed to survive was not goodwill between humans but rather the fear they had of each other, Hobbes claims.[3] In Machiavelli it is power – by which he means physical power, the ability to inflict physical violence and to have it inflicted on one – that creates the possibility of a society emerging.

Machiavelli had the best intentions with his political philosophy. Underlying it is a deep anthropological pessimism, where people will always prove to be evil unless external necessities force them to the opposite:

> They who lay the foundations of a State and furnish it with laws must, as is shown by all who have treated of civil government, and by examples of which history is full, assume that all men are bad, and will always, when they have free field, give loose to their evil inclinations; and that if these for a while remain hidden, it is owing to some secret cause, which, from our having no contrary experience, we do not recognize at once, but which is afterwards revealed by Time, of whom we speak as the father of all truth.[4]

With this as his basic premise, it follows fairly directly that a well-organized state must be built on coercion and a constant danger of violence. That the premise itself is extremely suspect is another matter that is not going to be discussed further here.[5] The aim of violence should be to ensure the continuance of the society. In *The Prince*, Machiavelli states:

> The good use of violence (to the extent that it is at all possible to speak of anything evil as being good) only occurs when one's own security calls for it and at a quick tempo. After which, it is stopped immediately, and one attempts to the greatest possible degree to be of use to one's subjects. The bad use of violence is long in duration and, although it has modest beginnings, it increases rather than decreases with time.[6]

Bad violence is that which has almost acquired a value in itself, and that therefore escalates. This form of violence, according to Machiavelli, is bad because it does not fulfil the function of violence, which is to secure social order via a strategic elimination of enemies and a suitable amount of fear. The ruler who resorts to bad violence spreads too much fear and thereby undermines his own regime: 'He will never be able to rely on his subjects, and they will never feel secure with him on account of his continuous use of violence.'[7] Such a ruler will not actually be the one who controls fear – and the control of fear is, as mentioned, the basis for the control of the state – but will rather become 'the victim of his own fear'.[8] Machiavelli stresses that a prince must not 'hesitate to make use of evil when conditions call for it', but also that a prince ought 'to cultivate the friendship of the people'.[9] He also writes that 'a prince must strive to be merciful and not cruel'.[10] It might seem that I am painting quite a rosy picture of Machiavelli, so let me emphasize once more that fear is what ultimately secures the prince's power and thereby the social order. Even if it is a good thing for a prince to be loved, it is more important for him to be feared, because fear goes deeper than love: 'Love is nothing else than a commitment that always ceases when people, in their wickedness, see a chance of feathering their own nest. The prince, on the other hand, is kept alive by the fear of punishment, which must always be maintained.'[11]

As Hobbes was to express it a century later, fear is the passion that must be taken into account in politics.[12] Hobbes based the state on the fear of death, or more precisely, on the fear of a *violent* death.[13] Hobbes's starting point is the idea of a natural state in which people lived without laws. The natural state is a fiction, the aim of which is to scare people. Such a state, according to Hobbes, would be characterized by 'every man for himself'. The natural state is a state of war. The reason for this lies in human nature: the struggle for self-preservation, riches and honour naturally leads people to be in conflict with each other.[14] Hobbes admittedly sees human beings as having a capacity for compassion, but this feeling is too weak to prevent constant conflicts. The crucial thing is not that people actually are in constant conflict with each other but the possibility that a conflict can always break out.[15]

People's intention is always to protect their own property, to seize that of others, and to gain recognition. The theory of a natural state is not meant to be an account of any real society but rather a model of how people would behave towards each other if there was no form of government to restrain them. In the natural state, people have no rights. This marks a strong break with the concept of natural rights that had dominated political theory since antiquity. In Hobbes's natural state there is only one right – the right to use every means to get what one wants. The only law of nature in the natural state is that of the strong over the weak.

The natural state is not a good state to live in. Even the strongest of the strong will always have to be on their guard, for many weak people can join forces and thus become stronger. You do not know if another person is a friend or an enemy – so, to be on the safe side, you must treat everyone else as a potential enemy. And you will be treated likewise. Thus the life of man is 'solitary, poor, nasty, brutish, and short.'[16] Fear becomes all-embracing, thereby undermining each individual's possibilities for realizing a positive vision of his life – life ends up as nothing but a cohesive defence against dangers that threaten from all sides. It is the worst of all possible worlds to live in. By installing a sovereign ruler, fear acquires a different order, where space is created for positive aims in life – and not only the avoidance of a painful death. So people choose to abandon their natural freedom in exchange for security, and this is something everyone does by making a social pact. We know, however, how little anyone's word is worth, so there has to be a supreme power that can sanction the pact. This is done by each individual member of society abrogating his right to self-determination to a single person, the sovereign, who has unlimited power. He has no duties towards his subjects, but they promise to do precisely as he says. The only thing he cannot demand is the lives of his subjects, for it was those he was appointed to protect in the first place. All the laws the sovereign makes are considered to be God's laws, but it is the sovereign who decides what God's laws are and what the state religion is to be.

The natural state Hobbes describes is one devoid of trust. The relationship between human beings is rather one of total mistrust. They are not held together by any 'social glue', as I characterized trust in the previous chapter, and are thus completely thrown upon themselves. When the ruler is installed, a relation of trust is at least established in one person, since one must assume that he will practise the power he has been allotted. Hereby, one can also gain indirect trust in one's fellow human beings, because they must be assumed to act in such a way that they do not call down the wrath of the ruler on their heads. Such an indirect trust, however, is something completely different from the natural, original trust described by, among others, Løgstrup. It is a perverted trust that is grounded in fear.

Fear can be an effective tool for maintaining order in a society. Hobbes underlines that no emotion makes people less likely to break the law than fear.[17] He also writes that fear makes people likely to live in peace with each other.[18] The state threatens punishment that outweighs the possible advantages of laying hands on other people's lives or property, and the fear of this punishment ensures that citizens can have a peaceful and ordered coexistence. This coexistence is possibly 'ordered', but can it be called a free society?

Kant distinguishes between fear and respect of the law as an underlying determiner of our actions, claiming that respect is to be preferred, precisely because it does not rob us of our freedom.[19] Hobbes, on the other hand, insists that acting out of fear can be fully reconciled with acting freely.[20] It could be argued, though, that this is a 'tamed' form of freedom. It could be said that Hobbes suggests that people will choose to exchange one type of fear for another. You replace a fear of everything with a fear of the sovereign ruler: total fear is replaced by a limited fear. For Hobbes, the task of the state is to ensure that people fear the 'right' things. In other words, fear is not an alien element in a civilized society, rather a necessary prerequisite for a civilized society being able to develop at all. Even though Hobbes, as mentioned, acknowledges that humans have a certain capacity for compassion, it is fear that in reality becomes the actual basis of morality. The crucial thing is that the state manages to direct fear in an appropriate way. It has to convince the people that certain things should be feared rather than others, since the people will not, just like that, fear what is appropriate from the point of view of the state. Hobbes points out that this can necessitate a certain amount of staging by the state, which magnifies certain phenomena and diminishes others.

Machiavelli had great confidence in the ability of the prince to govern via a fear that emanates from his ability to inflict violence on his subjects. Hobbes did not have the same belief that the sovereign ruler could govern by fear alone.[21] As Hobbes saw it, the subjects must also show a willingness to submit because they believe it furthers their interests. Political fear is thus not simply something that is inflicted on citizens from above. It is rather a collective process that involves willing individuals and social institutions such as the church. The individuals will monitor each other and warn each other of the consequences of contravening the social order. A tyranny – for that is what Hobbes was advocating – can hardly exist without all the citizens being aware that other citizens are monitoring them and can denounce them to the state.[22]

In Montesquieu's *The Spirit of Laws* (1748), on the other hand, fear of the despot is portrayed as the greatest problem. While fear of the ruler, according to Hobbes, served the citizens' interests, Montesquieu saw it exclusively as being an outcome of a despot's perverse lust for power. Therefore, it is the fear of despotic terror that is the most important justification of the principle of division of powers and the establishing of a liberal order. Montesquieu's political philosophy is also motivated by fear, but it is of a different nature than that of Hobbes. Alexis de Tocqueville, for his part, focused on the possibility of another type of despotic terror, where the tyrant is not an absolute ruler but a compact majority that undermines a liberal order on the basis of a fear that is the result of traditional authorities having lapsed.[23] Tocqueville was writing in the wake of the French Revolution, when the old European regimes had started to collapse. In this situation, people were less afraid of losing their lives as such – which was what Hobbes based his philosophy on – than of losing traditional truths, the absolute nature of moral values and so on. It could be said that they were afraid of modernity itself, as a state where they felt themselves threatened. They were afraid of the future, and in order to remedy this dread, Tocqueville believed that they would create a highly suppressive government that could create order and re-establish fixed norms.

Here a danger lurks for every government: that it complies with the fear of its citizens. The authorities are constantly on guard when the fear of a phenomenon grows. The reason for this is that this fear also undermines the legitimacy of the state, since this legitimacy rests quite fundamentally on the ability of the state to protect its citizens. This protection not only applies to its ability to prevent citizens from being exposed to violence from other citizens, military forces from another state or terrorists but also to illnesses and various phenomena that can constitute a health risk. If the state does not seem able to provide its citizens with this protection, it leads potentially to a destabilizing of the state. So the state must make it clear that it is combating that which causes the fear. The problem is that this can cause the fear to escalate, since the state has to legitimize its acts by referring to the danger that creates the fear. In order to bolster its legitimacy, these dangers will often be over-dramatized.

Fear has once more gained high status as a basis of political theory. The historian and journalist Michael Ignatieff argues that 'in the twentieth century, the idea of human universality rests less on hope than on fear, less on optimism about the human capacity for good than on dread of human capacity for evil, less on a vision of man as maker of his history than of man the wolf toward his own kind.'[24] The philosopher Judith Shklar advocates what she calls a 'liberalism of fear', a position that does not set up a positive goal we all ought to be striving towards but rather a negative vision we can all agree we ought to try to avoid. She feels that in a fragmentary age we can agree that terror, cruelty and suffering ought to be avoided.[25] Fear can have a cohesive effect – it can re-establish a sense of community that would seem to have been lost in the age of individualism. From Shklar's perspective, systematic fear is what makes political freedom possible. It must be pointed out here that the fear about which Shklar is writing is not just a fear for one's own welfare but also for that of one's fellow citizens.

Fear becomes a resource for the community. So it would seem that the maintenance of fear is a prerequisite for the continued existence of the community. This is well illustrated in M. Night Shyamalan's film *The Village* (2004). The inhabitants of a village live like American settlers in the nineteenth century. The village functions as a kind of enclosed unit, and there are frightening monsters in the forest that are so terrifying that they stop the inhabitants from wanting to leave the village. Towards the end of the film we see that the villagers are not living in the nineteenth century but are people from our own time, all of whom have been victims of the violent crimes of modern urbanism. They have established their own society outside the rest of society, and their society has a substantial number of various rules. These rules are based on a consciously constructed morality; not something based on older conventions or a natural right – it is a pure construct. It also transpires that the frightening monsters in the forest are illusions, created by 'the elders' in order to keep the young people inside the village. The idea of something terrifying 'out there' keeps their society together as a unit. There is, by the way, solid empirical evidence to support the idea that reminders of one's own mortality promotes nationalism and other forms of group identification.[26] So the fear of fear has an integrative effect on a group, but at the same time can promote animosity towards other groups.

It is difficult not to read Shyamalan's film as a comment on contemporary American society and politics. The burden is that one must obey the village rules, since only they can guarantee the security of the inhabitants. These rules, however, are also isolationist. The American writer Ralph Waldo Emerson warned against the evil that threatened the nation from without, claiming that the country had to consider itself as the source of virtue and stand alone in order to be victorious in this world.[27] This thought can be considered as an archetype in American politics.[28] *The Village* shows that the cultivation of fear 'out there' has a suppressive function. The fears maintain the village as a compact unit that is admittedly secure, but the price paid for this security is major limitations of individual freedom and a life that is lived in chronic fear.

What is often presented as a 'realistic' view of the political situation in the world today ought perhaps more to be described as a 'tabloid realism'.[29] It has a similar form of presentation to the tabloid newspapers, with sensational presentations of international politics. The presentation would seem to be governed by a wish to rouse the maximum amount of fear by conjuring up pictures of a violent anarchy that will destroy our entire civilization if firm political steps are not taken. This discourse began long before 11 September 2001. Perhaps the most-read book within the genre is Samuel Huntington's *The Clash of Civilisations* (1996), which argues that a major war between the West and other civilizations is not unlikely.[30] Even though Huntington is writing only about 'a potential threat', his choice of words is without a doubt designed to arouse fear. Other examples are articles and books by Zbigniew Brzezinski and Robert D. Kaplan.[31] All these books have become bestsellers, and have contributed to disseminating a particular view of the world where the West – especially the USA – is threatened from without. A recurring theme is that globalization and deterritorialization are undermining American security and sovereignty. The events of 9/11 are then seen as confirmation of the fact that these analyses were correct. The answer to the problem posed by these threats is then an increased emphasis on security and order, which then becomes the most important concern within home and foreign policy.

Fear is used as a tool for social control. What causes fear in citizens is not merely the terrorists that exist at some unspecified location but also public information about how dangerous these terrorists are. This information is then used to justify various measures that are to ensure the security of these same citizens. Political fear does not arise in a vacuum – it is created and maintained. Its function is to promote various political practices. Strong interests of a political and economic nature have considerably inflated the danger of terror.[32] In the US, the states are granted funding to combat terrorism that is based, among other things, on the number of terrorist targets in that state. This, of course, creates an incentive to report as many such targets as possible, in order to get more funding. The result becomes quite absurd. In the US as a whole there are officially 77,069 potential terrorist targets – the curious thing, though, is that the state of Indiana has 50% more terrorist targets than New York and twice as many as California.[33] The list includes an Amish-operated popcorn factory with five employees, a flea market in Sweetwater, ice-cream and doughnut stores, etc. Naturally, every location is in principle potentially a terrorist target, but the likelihood of any of these places attracting terrorists is modest to say the least. An internal review of the US Justice Department has also revealed considerable incorrect reporting in its anti-terror statistics over a number of years, with such things as drug-smuggling, illegal immigration and marital crimes being classified as terrorist-related.[34] Yet these misleading figures have been published and used as an indicator of the extent of the terrorist threat against the US. The figures have also been used as a basis for budget measures.

The political gains can also be considerable. George W. Bush has repeatedly claimed that 'the war against terror' is unlike all previous wars in US history, and that it will continue as far as can be foreseen. Given such an external threat, the only possible answer is a strong state. Here it is possible to imagine that the administration has listened to Machiavelli's advice that 'a wise prince ought to adopt such a course that his citizens will always in every sort and kind of circumstance have need of the state and of him, and then he will always find them faithful'.[35] As Machiavelli saw it, few methods are more effective than the spreading of fear. A clear correlation has been shown between warnings about terror from the Bush administration and support of the administration by the people.[36] This support was not only evident within the field of security policy but it also spread to other areas, such as economic policy. The announcement of terrorist threats gave a definite, immediate gain. During the 2004 presidential campaign, one of the Republican TV spots showed a pack of wolves in a dark forest, while the voice-over said that 'weakness attracts those who are waiting to do America harm'. The message was that there was a 'pack of wolves' out there, in the form of terrorists that would try to harm the US if Bush was not elected.

In Bush's state of the nation address on 28 January 2003, he claimed: 'in this century, the ideology of power and domination has appeared again, and seeks to gain the ultimate weapons of terror. Once again, this nation and all our friends are all that stand between a world at peace, and a world of chaos and constant alarm.'[37] He asked his audience to imagine the nineteen hijackers from 9/11 equipped with weapons from Saddam Hussein's arsenals, and claimed that such a combination would surpass all the horrors the nation had ever known. Via more or less systematic disinformation, a majority of the American population was actually convinced that Iraq was behind 9/11. In surveys conducted in January and February 2003, 72% of those asked believed that Saddam had personally been involved in the attack, and 44% believed that 'most' or 'some' of the hijackers were Iraqi citizens.[38] This was remarkable, since practically no one had mentioned Iraq in surveys immediately after the attack. In the intervening period, an image of Saddam as the prime source of the terrorist threat facing the US had been created, and this image was used to legitimize the Iraq war to the American people. This image proved to be amazingly difficult to correct: in July 2006, 64% still believed that Saddam had had 'strong links' to Al-Qaeda, and 50% were convinced that Saddam had had weapons of mass destruction.[39] The tide would seem to be changing, however: in a survey from February 2007, 63% of Americans asked said that they did not trust the reliability of the information coming from the Bush administration about the nature of the threat being presented.[40]

I do not intend to discuss the legitimacy of US warfare during recent years to any great extent. The invasion of Afghanistan was, in my opinion, legitimate.[41] On the other hand, the invasion of Iraq was a mistake according to most yardsticks, even though there is no reason to regret Saddam Hussein's removal from power. The most important part of the official justification of the invasion of Iraq was that Saddam was in possession of nuclear weapons, although it is a trifle curious that the country in 'the axis of evil' that actually did not have a nuclear programme was the one that was invaded – though the other states demonstrably had. The possible spread of nuclear weapons to new states is a real danger, and, as far as can be judged, a far greater danger than the more modest likelihood of terrorist organizations gaining possession of such weapons, but from such a perspective, Iraq was a very strange target. The war was justified by lies, constituted a violation of international law, and has not only inflicted great suffering on the Iraqi population but has also been one of the most important reasons why radical Islamic movements have had a greater number of recruits than ever before. The 'war against terror' has so far had made the world a much less safe place. This is confirmed in reports from the US's own intelligence agencies.[42] Secretary of Defence Donald Rumsfeld stated that the war against terror would have been won when Americans could once more feel secure – in that case, it would seem that a war is being fought that cannot be won.

An obvious problem about the 'fight against terror', understood as a fight against fear, is that it undoubtedly increases fear by insisting on the danger all of us find ourselves in. In the *National Strategy for Combating Terrorism*

(2003) terrorism is described as an 'evil that is intent on threatening and destroying our basic freedoms and our way of life'.[43] It 'threatens the very idea of civilised society'.[44] The US is considered to be the power that guarantees world order and peace – and therefore every threat against the US is a threat against the world as a whole. Consequently, everything that the US does to defend itself against terrorism will be justified by the argument that it is necessary if the world as we know it will be able to continue to exist at all . It is portrayed as a fight between freedom and fear, where the US represents freedom and terrorism fear.[45] The representatives of fear are spread all over the world; therefore, those of freedom must be correspondingly global in their fight against fear. The world as a whole comes under the US's jurisdiction, and every act of terror becomes a threat against the US and against world peace as a whole, no matter where this act takes place. It is also considered sufficient for these threats to be *possible*. In a speech at West Point military academy, Bush said: 'If we wait for threats to fully materialize, we will have waited too long.'[46] In other words, he uses a better-safe-than-sorry principle, as he has done in many other areas. Here he is supported by such a thinker as Michael Ignatieff, who claims that if we do not identify, track down and eradicate the terrorists now, they may become extremely dangerous and eventually acquire weapons of mass destruction.[47]

There is, however, a paradox in the US's fight against terrorism. On the one hand, the US considers itself the guarantor of the continued existence of peace and liberal values, and on the other the country's own actions are exempt from these values in the fight to preserve them. The idea is that the men of violence, the terrorists, place themselves outside the moral order via their actions, and it must then also be permissible for the person defending himself to do the same – as long as the US is threatened by terrorism, the country is therefore in principle not bound by the norms the state as its point of departure seeks to defend. This is reminiscent of the sovereign in Hobbes.[48] In Hobbes, all citizens are subject to a contract that gives the sovereign unlimited powers to govern the state as he sees fit. The social contract is absolutely binding on all citizens, but the sovereign himself is not subject to the contract that he undertakes to guarantee. Similarly, the US is conceived as being the guarantor of a civilized world, as the country that can maintain a moral order, but that stands outside this order. Just as little as the subjects of Hobbes's sovereign can complain about what he undertakes can one complain that the US does what it deems 'necessary' to combat 'the enemies of freedom'.

As Ulrich Beck points out, the very antithesis of the new liberalism, the Hobbesian principle of an omnipresent state, appeared as a guarantee of security.[49] To a great extent it can be claimed that the Bush administration tacitly has followed the view of the German lawyer and philosopher Carl Schmitt that liberalism does not have any solutions to offer in a time of crisis. A strong state is what is called for. Schmitt argues that 'Every religious, morally economic, ethnical or other conflict changes into a political conflict when it is strong enough to effectively group people as friends or foes.'[50] Schmitt extracts dramatic consequences from this. For him, the political itself is defined by the division into friend and foe. A political act consists in maintaining one's own existence and destroying those that threaten it, and there is little room for overcoming conflicts via discussion. Such political action is the sole right of the state, and in order to maintain itself the state must also eliminate all enemies within, that is, all those who do not fit into a homogenous unity. Every genuine political theory, according to Schmitt, must assume that man is evil, that man is a dangerous being. It is here, in the fear of what humans can do to each other, that the state finds the justification of its own existence – the ability of the state to protect one is the argument for submitting to it.

Schmitt would say that the terrorist threat made the state aware of its own true being. Schmitt would, however, have considered subsequent developments as worrying, since there has been increasing pressure to make states opposing terrorism conform to the same set of norms as all others, where supreme court measures have concluded that prisoners in the war against terror are to be protected by the Geneva Convention and that they are to be guaranteed far greater legal rights. As a reply to this challenge, the British defence minister, John Reid, gave a dramatic speech at the Royal United Services Institute in April 2006, where he claimed that the threat from terrorists who can make use of weapons of mass destruction is so serious that one can no longer adhere to the rules stated in the Geneva Convention. There are examples – especially in South and Latin America – of successful military campaigns against terrorism. The problem is that the means used in these cases are completely unacceptable to a liberal democracy.

We have seen serious restrictions on freedom in the country that has normally felt itself to be the true incarnation of personal freedom, that is, the US. We have seen many examples of apparently arbitrary arrests – in many cases with subsequent incarceration – of people, especially Muslims, both inside and outside the US. Completely elementary principles of legal rights have been disregarded. The anti-terror policy has, however, affected more than Muslims – it has also led to serious encroachments on the liberty of other American citizens.[51] References to the security of the nation are used in order to forbid the formation of trade unions among employees in public administration and at airports and ports. Among the most serious encroachments is the comprehensive phone-tapping that the National Security Agency (NSA) has carried out without any court order. A large number of American citizens stated in a questionnaire that they considered the limitations imposed on their civil rights to be completely legitimate. The threat of terror was perceived as being so serious that the loss of civil rights was less important.

Critics of such encroachments on civil rights are met, among other things, by the following utterance from Attorney General John Ashcroft: 'To those who scare peace-loving people with phantoms of lost liberty, my message is this', he said. 'Your tactics only aid terrorists, for they erode our national unity and diminish our resolve. They give ammunition to America's enemies, and pause to America's friends. They encourage people of good will to remain silent in the face of evil.' When George W. Bush was confronted with the illegal programme of phone-tapping, he answered: 'The fact that we're discussing this program is helping the enemy.'[52] The criticism made this almost synonymous with having an 'unpatriotic' attitude, and several of the most important premises for a functioning democracy were undermined.[53] As a counterweight to the rhetoric of the Bush administration it is tempting to quote one of the founding fathers, Benjamin Franklin: 'They who would give up an essential liberty for temporary security, deserve neither liberty or security.'[54]

What, then, is the threat that justifies these dramatic encroachments on civil rights? In short: what is terrorism? This question is not all that easy to answer, since there is no internationally recognized definition of 'terrorism'. In recent years, the use of the concept 'terrorist' has become so broad that it seems to include most of the armed resistance movements that have ever existed – and more besides. The word is used to describe practically all political resorting to violence not sanctioned by the state. On the basis of such a definition, George Washington, for example, would have been a terrorist in his fight against the British. And the whole issue becomes even more problematic when states are also stamped as being terrorist states, as when the Bush administration accused Saddam Hussein's Iraq of committing 'acts of terror' against its own people. This use of the concept of terror is not new – it is in fact the oldest use, one that dates back to Robespierre's 'terror' – but it means that the concept has so wide a use that it becomes uninformative. Clearer criteria are called for.

The researcher into terror Louise Richardson lists seven criteria for an act to be classified as 'terrorism':

1 The act is politically motivated.
2 The act involves violence or the threat of violence.
3 The aim of the act is not to defeat the enemy but to convey a message.
4 The act and the aim of it (the victim) often have a symbolic significance.
5 The act is not committed by a state but by a group at a lower level.
6 The victims and target group of the act are not identical.
7 The act consciously targets civil victims.[55]

Several of these criteria are problematic. Individual states, for example, have been so deeply involved in acts of terror that criterion 5 can seem to be unreasonable. Criterion 7 can also be questioned, since it excludes the possibility that an attack on a military target can be considered as terrorism (it must in that case be classified as a guerrilla attack).[56] Let us here focus on the idea that it has to do with violence, the primary aim of which is to spread fear. It is violence directed against a public, and not first and foremost against those directly affected by the acts. A crucial part of the 'secret' of terrorism, that it can have such a major effect using very limited means, is because of the apparent randomness with which it strikes. Random violence is more frightening than violence aimed at selected, specific victims: if no particular people are chosen as a target, no one can feel safe either. By striking more or less at random, though preferably symbolically important targets, fear is created in as many citizens as possible.

The extent to which a person, group or act may be placed in the category of 'terrorism' is a question of the means that are used, and what one expects to achieve by these means. The typical terrorist is completely convinced that he or she has a just cause, and as such is a typical instance of what I have earlier referred to as 'idealistic evil'.[57] A player can also have a just cause and yet also be a terrorist. Very few people now think of Nelson Mandela as a terrorist, but for a long time he was considered a terrorist by the authorities in most Western countries. Even Amnesty International refused for a long time to recognize Mandela as a prisoner of conscience, since he had been convicted for violence. Using the broad definitions of terrorism that have been employed in most Western states in recent years, it is clear that Mandela's activities prior to his incarceration fall within that definition. It does not alter the case that Mandela undoubtedly preferred non-violent to violent means when he also claimed that violent means could be necessary for political change. This was a view Mandela always maintained, and even in the speech he gave when released on 11 February 1990 he said that the armed struggle of the ANC was not over, and that the factors that had made it necessary to establish the military wing of the ANC in 1960 still existed. Another example of a former terrorist who later won the Nobel Peace Prize is the former prime minister of Israel Menachem Begin, who shared the award with Anwar Sadat in 1978.

I do not intend to dwell here on the question of which types of political violence are legitimate and which are illegitimate,[58] since I am more interested in the role fear plays as a political tool. The struggle against the causes of fear becomes something that itself produces fear. If the authorities constantly underline – and exaggerate – the danger of terror that citizens are exposed to, it is in fact possible to claim that the state too is terrorizing its citizens.[59] A symbiosis arises between terrorists and authorities, since while being at odds with each other they both produce the same result: a population that lives in fear. And both exploit this fear politically. An important part of our political freedom is precisely to be able to live our lives without too much fear. A government that promotes fear, by creating an exaggerated impression of everyone being in danger of exposure to a terrorist attack, for example, thereby limits the freedom of its citizens. The core concept of liberal democracies is a respect of individual autonomy – and fear harms this autonomy.

Is it reasonable to claim that the authorities are exaggerating the danger of terrorism? It would definitely seem so if we take a sober look at how many people have actually been affected by terrorist attacks. In 1999, 233 people were killed by terrorists on a global basis, and five of the victims were Americans. In 2000, the global figure was 405, of which 19 were Americans.[60] Viewed thus, there is an enormous leap to 2001, where the 11 September attack was on an extreme scale. Almost ten times as many people were killed than in any previous terrorist attack, which makes it problematic to consider this attack as a typical example of terrorism. Most terrorist attacks do not claim so many lives. The gas attack on the Tokyo subway in March 1995, which used sarin, one of the most toxic substances on this earth, claimed twelve lives. The major attack on the railway in Madrid in March 2004 claimed 191 human lives, while the attacks in London on 7 and 21 July 2005 claimed a total of 56 lives, including those of the four suicide bombers. Compared with most other causes of death, terrorist attacks are not what ought to concern us most.

About 3,000 North Americans were killed by terrorists in the course of 2001 and, no matter how terrible that is, we ought also to remember that in the same year 700,000 North

Americans died of heart-related illnesses and 550,000 of cancer. Another possible comparison is this: six times as many Americans were killed by drunken drivers as by terrorists in 2001. If you add up the numbers of those killed in various terrorist attacks of the last decades, the total is not all that high. Naturally, one ought to wish that none of these lives had been lost, but the point here is that the probability of being killed in a terrorist attack is so small that you have to be particularly unlucky to be a victim. Even though the danger of a terrorist attack must not be underestimated, an attempt must be made to give as reasonable a picture as possible of the extent of this danger. Based on such a 'reasonable picture', it is difficult to see that the 'war against terror' has sensible proportions.

Obviously, terrorism must be combated, but in my opinion it is just as obvious that the necessity of doing so is insufficient to justify the disregarding of basic rights. We must be able to demand that the 'war against terror' respects the values and institutions it claims to be protecting. We also ought to recall that the main purpose of the 11 September terrorists was not to inflict material damage on the West but psychological damage. The material damage on the highly symbolic buildings – and the almost 3,000 people killed – was nothing else than a means of inculcating fear in the West. As such, they could hardly have had greater success. A great deal of this success they can thank Western authorities and media for, since the exaggeration of the danger of terrorism has given fear proportions the terrorists could never have achieved on their own.

A state that legitimizes itself and ensures the obedience of its citizens by the use of fear is not basically creating a democracy, since the strategy of fear undermines the liberty that is the core of democracy. Precisely because it is legitimized via fear one can claim that 'the war against terror' is a greater danger to democracy than terrorism itself. As the philosopher Michael Walzer points out, the liberalism of fear presupposes a liberalism of hope. The reason is that what we fear for is everything we value positively.[61] Freedom and justice must be ascribed a more fundamental role than fear in our political thinking. Then much of 'the war against terror' will be seen in a dubious light, since it has based itself so strongly on fear and disregarded freedom and justice. Not only has it led to concrete changes in citizens' civil rights; it has also promoted a climate of fear that in itself undermines our freedom. The fight against the causes of fear itself causes fear. A crucial part of our political freedom consists precisely in living our lives without too much fear.

SEVEN

Beyond Fear?

Fear is the main source of superstition, and one of the
main sources of cruelty. To conquer fear is the beginning of
wisdom, in the pursuit of truth as in the endeavour after a
worthy manner of life.

Bertrand Russell, *An Outline of Intellectual Rubbish*

The psychoanalyst Adam Phillips tells a joke about a mullah standing outside his house in London, scattering grains of maize.[1] An Englishman walks over and asks him why he is doing this. 'To keep the tigers away', the mullah replies. The Englishman objects that there aren't any tigers. 'That means it works', says the mullah.

The fact that we are *not* struck down by a given misfortune is no guarantee that we actually have a sensible attitude towards it. Fear tells us very little indeed about the object of that fear. The fact that a person or a society does certain things to protect itself against a danger says little about the nature of that danger. Our fear probably says more about us than about what we fear. That we fear something does not necessarily mean that we *ought* to fear it. But simply because something is feared, authorities tend to introduce measures that often erode our freedom – and without our necessarily becoming any more secure as a result.[2] The fact that someone is afraid of a risk is not in itself a sufficient reason for authorities to seek to reduce that risk. If it is insignificant, the authorities ought to confine themselves to inform the person precisely that. Similarly, the authorities ought to intervene if there is a serious risk, even though the majority of the population might be completely unworried.

There will always be plenty to fear. In the post-war years, until 1989, the threat came from Communism. That was replaced by the threat against the environment, and during recent years terrorism has grabbed the headlines. The object of fear changes, but it would be an illusion to believe that we could live in a world without fear. We ought, however, to realize that our fear is not an objective reflection of reality, and there are strong interests that control the directions our fear takes. Fear is one of the most important power factors that exists, and the person that can control its direction in a society has gained considerable power over that society. We can perhaps say, along with the philosopher Giorgio Agamben, that we live today in a permanent state of emergency, where the reference to serious dangers almost works like a trump card – and the card trumps recognized democratic rights.[3]

Perhaps the most often quoted statement on fear comes from Franklin D. Roosevelt's 1933 speech, when the Great Depression was at its height, in which he said: 'The only thing we have to fear is fear itself.' It was a true message, since the nation was in an apparently bottomless crisis. So he has to be forgiven that the formulation was not completely original, as versions of it can be found in, among others, Montaigne and Thoreau. The point is a good one, nevertheless. We ought to fear fear because it undermines so much of what is really important in our lives.

It is easy to agree with the assertion made by the author and Nobel Prize winner Wole Soyinka that humanity ought rather to attempt to resolve the climate of fear with which we surround ourselves than live in it.[4] The question is how to set about it. Mass media, authorities and pressure groups must be asked to behave more responsibly when it comes to fear – not to over-dramatize dangers, no matter how 'good' their intentions. Health authorities ought not to use exaggerated scare propaganda in order to combat smoking and drugs, for example. The mass media ought not to use banner headlines to warn people of the danger of eating this or that, if these dangers are in fact infinitesimal. Pressure groups ought not to exaggerate a present danger just to get media coverage. It is, however, doubtful whether they will assume such a responsibility, since inflicting fear on others is perhaps the most effective tool all of them have in order to gain their respective objectives – whether that is to improve public health, sell newspapers or draw people's attention to environmental problems.

As long as fear works excellently as a sales item for the mass media, it is improbable that they will adopt a more responsible attitude. We ought to be aware of the fact, however, that scare campaigns can have serious consequences. In the news coverage of the situation in New Orleans after Hurricane Katrina in 2005 we can find a crass example of a lack of accordance between reality and the horror scenarios of the mass media. CNN talked about snipers firing at rescue helicopters, and that there were gangs moving from one district to another, raping every victim they came across. FOX News adopted the same line. The talkshow queen Oprah Winfrey had a special broadcast in which guests talked about babies being raped, and Winfrey confirmed that there were gangs that were better armed than the police. Some people even went so far as to report cannibalism. The refrain was that New Orleans was in a totally lawless state, where killing and rape were the rule rather than the exception. It is understandable that rescue crews were not eager to enter such a zone. So the evacuation of patients from hospitals was postponed – which resulted in a number of people dying. Ambulances ceased driving until order could be restored once more. The military personnel that entered took many safety precautions, something that delayed their rescue operation considerably. Many police simply stopped, fearing what they might encounter in the city, and the remaining police were diverted to stopping the murderous gangs instead of helping in the rescue operation. The problem of all this was that these orgies of violence never took place at all.[5] New Orleans has normally had fairly high statistics of violence, but it looks as if there was an actual *decline* in violence during the disaster. What people did – and this was most understandable – was to steal food and drink and other necessities from shops in order to stay alive. Apart from that, it looks as if the population of the disaster-stricken city behaved in an exemplary way. All information about the apparently lawless state of affairs led to human lives being lost. This is a clear example of the crisis-maximizing mode of the mass media in no way being an innocent phenomenon – it causes concrete damage. This example clearly shows – not least – the total lack of trust the world had that people would behave in a morally responsible manner in a crisis situation.

We seem to be culturally disposed to assume negative consequences, and we have a fluid fear that is chronically hunting for new objects it can link up with.[6] Such a frightening world is not a happy one. A general perception among people is that we are exposed to a greater risk today than previously, and that this tendency is only going to get worse. A decisive factor in people's perception of their own happiness is their assumptions about the future. People who live in miserable circumstances, but who believe that things will improve, generally speaking are more content than those with a higher standard of living who think they will fare worse in the future. Worries about the future can overshadow the present. But we have probably never had fewer real grounds for concern.

The spreading of fear undermines our ontological security, that is, the basic security we must have in order to be able to function well in our everyday lives. In a risk culture, all of us are victims. We become pathetic, in the sense that we become 'sufferers', passive recipients. Fear robs us of our freedom. The freedom that can normally be taken for granted in everyday life is lessened by insecurity. As Wole Soyinka says, 'caution and calculation replace a norm of spontaneity or routine'.[7] This spontaneity is a vital part of our freedom. The person who constantly has to think about his actions, even quite humdrum, ordinary things, has lost some of his free sphere of action. This may have to do with newspaper articles about acts of violence in one's neighbourhood, that terrorists can strike 'anywhere and at any time', that the food we eat is unsafe or that a dangerous virus is spreading fast. When we are influenced by such information, we lose some of our everyday spontaneity.

It is not good to live in fear. As Montaigne points out: 'I will become familiar with sufferings soon enough, without needing to prolong them by the evil known as dread. The man who fears suffering, is already suffering from fear.'[8] It is difficult to imagine that all fear will ever completely disappear. Joseph Conrad puts it thus:

> Fear always remains. A man may destroy everything within himself, love and hate and belief, and even doubt; but as long as he clings to life he cannot destroy fear: the fear, subtle, indestructible, and terrible, that pervades his being; that tinges his thoughts; that lurks in his heart; that watches on his lips the struggle of his last breath.[9]

This formulation exaggerates the role of fear in human life, since fear is portrayed as still being the basic thing when everything else perishes. The role that fear plays in our lives also depends on the role we *allow* it to play. It is possible for us to try and counteract the *routine* that fear imposes, and we can try to replace it by hope.

Even though I advocate hope rather than fear, this does not mean that I wish for the return of the great social utopias. On the contrary, I believe that the fear society is a product of utopian thinking. 'Utopia' means, literally, a 'non-place', but people like to think of it as a 'good place', that is, as a 'eutopia' (the Greek prefix *eu-* meaning 'good' and *topos* meaning 'place'). As it says in Aldous Huxley's *Brave New World*, 'There isn't any need for a civilized man to bear anything that's seriously unpleasant.'[10] Utopias are societies that, by definition, do not contain fear. Precisely against this background, fear becomes so intolerable, and every misfortune so unacceptable.

When one reads about utopias, they have a tendency to appear to be completely unliveable in. It is as if *life* itself has been eliminated from these allegedly perfect societies. It looks as if our utopia is to create a society where all dangers are completely under control and misfortunes something we only can read about in history books. Could we manage to live in such a society? In the satirical tale *Running Wild* (1988), J. G. Ballard describes a small local community outside London that is completely under surveillance and protection.[11] One day, all the adults have been murdered and all the children have disappeared. We follow Richard Greville, a psychiatrist who works for the police, in his attempts to solve the mystery. He gradually works out that the children have not been kidnapped, but have murdered their parents before taking flight. The question is: why? There is no reason to believe that the parents have abused the children sexually or anything like that, that they have done anything else than try to create the best life possible for their children. The conclusion Greville finally comes to is startling: the children revolted against their parents and murdered them in order to escape from their smothering care. In an attempt to give the children a perfect, secure childhood, the parents had actually stolen their childhood from them.[12] Furthermore, it is clear that one has to have a fairly depressive view of reality 'out there' even to consider creating such a closed, risk-free society.

A culture of fear is a pessimistic culture. In Chuck Palahniuk's novel *Invisible Monsters* (1999), it says at one point: 'When did the future . . . switch from being a promise to a threat?'[13] We find examples of pessimistic depictions of the future as far back as antiquity, but the concept 'pessimism' does not begin to be used before the 1770s.[14] Great pessimism about the future would seem generally speaking to have been a marginal phenomenon earlier. Today, on the other hand, pessimism seems to have become quite commonly accepted, and the idea of progress is considered insane naivety.[15] Zygmunt Bauman writes:

> 'Progress' does not denote a quality of history, but the self-confidence of the present. The most profound, perhaps the only meaning with progress comprises two closely related convictions, namely that 'time is on our side', and that we are the ones who 'make things happen' . . . for people to are confident of their own power to change things, 'progress' is automatic. People who feel that things slip from their hands will never come up with the idea of progress, and it would seem ludicrous if it was voiced.[16]

In a culture of victims and fear, the concept of progress is an impossibility. The most one can get oneself to believe is that it is perhaps possible to prevent everything from getting even worse. If one does not experience the feeling of having a grip on existence and lacks confidence in being able to make the world a better place, the future is not all that enticing.

At the very beginning of his gigantic work on hope, Ernst Bloch explains that:

> The crucial thing is to learn to hope. Hope's work does not die away, it falls in love with succeeding rather than failing. Hope is superior to fear because it is neither passive nor caught up in nothingness. The effect of hope broadens people rather than restricts them.[17]

It is not a question of eradicating fear. Fear will always be there, but perhaps that means only that there is something that *means* something to us here in this life. What rouses fear is what in some way or other threatens the wishes one has for one's own life and the lives of others. The philosopher F. H. Bradley pointed out: 'The man who has ceased to fear has ceased to care.'[18] Fear, though, can be so comprehensive that it ruins much of what gives meaning to our lives, and can have a smothering effect. Hope, on the other hand, is optimistic, trusting, active and liberating. Hope can lift us up, while fear drags us down.

I do not claim that we live in 'the best of all possible worlds', but it could have been a lot worse – and it has been so for the greater part of human history. If we could freely choose a point in the history of mankind where we would want to live, right now would probably be an optimum choice. Our fear is the problem that comes with our luxury: we live such secure lives that we can worry about innumerable dangers that have practically no chance of making an impact on our lives. Our age naturally has to face a number of serious challenges: poverty, starvation, climate changes, political and religious conflicts, and so on. What we need is faith in human ability to try and solve these problems step by step, to learn from our mistakes and to create a better world – in short, a humanistic optimism.

References

Preface

1 Roland Barthes, *Lysten ved teksten*, trans. Arne Kjell Haugen (Oslo 1990), p. 48, from *Le Plaisir du texte* (Paris, 1973).

ONE The Culture of Fear

1 See, for example, Frank Furedi, *Culture of Fear: Risk-taking and the Morality of Low Expectation* (London and New York, 2005), and Joanna Bourke, *Fear: A Cultural History* (London, 2005).
2 Ludwig Wittgenstein, *Tractatus logico-philosophicus: Werkausgabe in 8 Bänden* (Frankfurt am Main, 1984), I, § 6.43.
3 Jean-Paul Sartre, *The Emotions: Outline of a Theory*, trans. B. Frechtman (New York, 1986), p. 87.
4 Michel de Montaigne, 'Forsvarstale for Raymond Sebond', in *Essays: Første bok*, trans. Beate Vibe (Oslo, 2005), p. 220.
5 Genesis 3:10.
6 Cf. Niklas Luhmann, *Risk: A Sociological Theory*, trans. Rhodes Barrett (New York, 1993).
7 Furedi, *Culture of Fear*, p. xii.
8 The figures for the occurrence of 'fear' over the past decade are:

1996	3,331	2002	4,709
1997	3,319	2003	4,757
1998	3,774	2004	4,443
1999	3,821	2005	5,308
2000	4,163	2006	5,883
2001	5,168		

I have limited myself to the years 1996–2006, since various newspapers have been included in the database at various points, and a search prior to 1996 – when *Dagbladet*, among others, was included in the database – cannot simply be compared with searches from 1996 and later. There is also a difference in the number of searchable sources from 1996 to 2006, and clearly such an overview based on occurrences in an *a-text* does not provide a fully reliable picture, although the database can at least be used to indicate an overall trend.

9 *Aftenposten*, 11 August 2005.
10 Cf. Paul Slovic, *The Perception of Risk* (London, 2000), chap. 8.
11 Ibid., chap. 13.
12 See, for example, Cass R. Sunstein, *Risk and Reason: Safety, Law and the Environment* (Cambridge, 2002), p. 4.
13 See Eric Howeler, 'Anxious Architectures: The Aesthetics of Surveillance', *Archis*, 3 (2002), and Eric Howeler, 'Paranoia Chic: The Aesthetics of Surveillance', *Loud Paper*, 3 (2004).
14 Sibylla Brodzinsky, 'Bulletproof Clothing that's Fashionable Too', *Business 2.0 Magazine*, 17 August 2006.
15 Paola Antonelli, *Safe: Design Takes on Risk*, Museum of Modern Art (New York, 2005), p. 80.
16 Ibid., p. 118.
17 Ibid., p. 15.
18 Nan Ellin, ed., *Architecture of Fear* (New York, 1997).
19 Melinda Muse, *I'm Afraid, You're Afraid: 448 Things to Fear and Why* (New York, 2000).
20 Jared Dimond, *Collapse: How Societies Choose to Fail or Succeed* (New York, 2004); James Howard Kunstler, *The Long Emergency: Surviving the End of Oil, Climate Change, and Other Converging Catastrophes of the Twenty-First Century* (New York, 2005); Eugene Linden, *The Winds of Change: Climate, Weather and the Destruction of Civilizations* (New York, 2006).
21 Matthew Stein, *When Technology Fails: A Manual for Self-*

Reliance and Planetary Survival (White River Junction, VT, 2000); Jack A. Spigarelli, *Crisis Preparedness Handbook: A Complete Guide to Home Storage and Physical Survival*, 2002).

22 Henrik Svensen, *Enden er nær: En bok om naturkatastrofer og samfunn* (Oslo, 2006), p. 15. Cf. p. 172; English edition *The End is Nigh: A History of Natural Disasters* (forthcoming London, 2009). The italics are original.

23 A spectre that has haunted the Internet has to do with the allegedly dangerous substance *dihydrogen monoxide* (see en.wikipedia.org/wiki/Dihydrogen_monoxide_hoax). If one looks at the dangerous effects of this substance, there are indeed reasons for concern: (1) It causes many deaths every year. (2) It is highly habit-forming, and abstinence symptoms can kill a person in a few days. (3) A large intake of the substance in liquid form can poison a person, resulting in death. (5) In gas form the substance can lead to serious burns. (6) The substance is often found in cancer tumours. (7) It also has the name 'hydroxylic acid', which is one of the main ingredients of acid rain. (8) It contributes to soil erosion and the greenhouse effect. A substance with so many dangerous effects apparently ought to be subject to rigorous control, or even banned. For this reason, many people have signed petitions calling for its prohibition. The problem is that the substance being described is ordinary *water*.

24 In connection with the twentieth anniversary of the Chernobyl disaster, many environmental activists and organizations took the opportunity to spread striking figures concerning the extent of the accident, the aim being to scare us from even considering nuclear power as a source of energy. Greenpeace published a report that claimed that the number of deaths and incidences of cancer had been seriously underestimated. According to Greenpeace, 270,000 people in Belarus will contract cancer as a result of the accident, and 93,000 of these will die of the disease. Greenpeace also estimates that 60,000 Russians have died as a result of

the accident and that the total number of deaths for the Ukraine and Belarus can reach a further 140,000. (*The Chernobyl Catastrophe. Consequences on Human Health,* Greenpeace, Amsterdam 2006: www.greenpeace.org/raw/ content/international/press/eports/chernobylhealthreport.pdf.) These figures were quoted quite uncritically by most mass media, despite the fact that the figures diverge considerably from those of WHO and The International Atomic Energy Agency, which estimate that between 4,000 and 9,000 people will eventually die (*Chernobyl's Legacy: Health, Environmental and Socio-Economic Impact,* IAEA, Vienna: www.iaea.org/ Publications/Booklets/Chernobyl/chernobyl.pdf.). Immediately after the accident, about 30 people died, and so far around 100 people have died for certain, although this figure will eventually reach several thousand. These figures, however, are far from those of Greenpeace, for which there is little or no independent support, and which it would seem have been vastly inflated in order to gain attention and funding for the organization. For the Greenpeace figures to have any credibility, small amounts of radition must have several times more dramatic an effect than we have any reason to believe.

25 Lee Jones, 'Turning Children Green with Fear', *Spiked*, 12 March 2007 www.spiked-online.com/index.php?/site/ article/2950/

26 Bourke, *Fear: A Cultural History*, p. 259.

27 For a presentation that takes this threat particularly seriously, but which can hardly be said to have made it seem likely, see Graham Allison, 'The Ongoing Failure of Imagination', *Bulletin of the Atomic Scientists*, LXII/5 (2006).

28 For a readable presentation of how the gas attack on the Tokyo subway in March 1995 was experienced by those involved, and how their lives changed after the attack, see Haruki Murakami, *Underground: The Tokyo Gas Attack and the Japanese Psyche*, trans. Alfred Birnbaum and Philip Gabriel (London, 2003).

29 See Human Security Centre, *Human Security Report 2005 – War and Peace in the 21st Century* (Oxford, 2006).

30 Furedi, *Culture of Fear*, p. vii.

31 For a comprehensive study of this, the emphasis being on American conditions, see David L. Altheide, *Creating Fear: News and the Construction of Crisis* (New York, 2002).

32 Cf. George Gerbner, 'Violence and Terror in and by the Media', in *Media, Crisis and Democracy: Mass Communication and the Disruption of Social Order*, ed. M. Raboy and B. Dagenais (London, 1992).

TWO What is Fear?

1 For a highly readable presentation and discussion of various theories about the emotions, the emphasis being on a cognitivist perspective, see Frode Nyeng, *Følelser – i filosofi, vitenskap og dagligliv* (Oslo, 2006). Most useful, in my opinion, is Robert Solomon, *The Passions: Emotions and the Meaning of Life* (Indianapolis and Cambridge, 1993).

2 Paul Ekman, 'An Argument for Basic Emotions', *Cognition and Emotion*, 6 (1992).

3 See Andrew Ortony et al., *The Cognitive Structure of the Emotions* (Cambridge, 1998), p. 27.

4 For a readable summary and discussion of the debate about 'basic emotions', see Robert C. Solomon, 'Back to Basics: On the Very Idea of "Basic Emotions"', in *Not Passion's Slave: Emotions and Choice* (Oxford, 2003).

5 Maurice Merleau-Ponty, *Phenomenology of Perception*, trans. Colin Smith (London, 1989), p. 184.

6 Ibid., p. 189.

7 Cf. Joanna Bourke, *Fear: A Cultural History* (London, 2005), p. 19.

8 For a study that has such a perspective, see Daniel M. Gross, *The Secret History of Emotion: From Aristotle's Rhetoric to*

Modern Brain Science (Chicago, 2006).

9   Cf. William M. Reddy, *The Navigation of Feeling: A Framework for the History of Emotion* (Cambridge, 2001), p. 12.

10 Michel de Montaigne, 'Om drukkenskap', in *Essays: Annen bok*, trans. Beate Vibe (Oslo, 2005), p. 28, and oregonstate.edu/instruct/phl302/texts/montaigne/montaigne-essays—2.html.

11 David Hume, *A Treatise of Human Nature* (London, 1984), book 2.9, p. 491.

12 Cf. Antonio Damasio, *Følelsen av hva som skjer: Kroppens og emosjonenes betydning for bevisstheten*, trans. Kåre A. Lie (Oslo, 2002), pp. 68–72.

13 Cf. Reiner Sprengelmeyer et al., 'Knowing no fear', *Proceedings of the Royal Society: Biological Sciences*, 1437 (1999).

14 Joseph LeDoux, *The Emotional Brain* (London, 1998).

15 Cf. Hans Selye, *The Stress of Life* (New York, 1976).

16 LeDoux, *The Emotional Brain*, p. 302.

17 Michael Meyer, *Philosophy and the Passions: Towards a History of Human Nature*, trans. Robert F. Barsky (Philadelphia, PA, 2000), p. 1.

18 Cf. Mohan Matthen, 'Biological Universals and the Nature of Fear', *Journal of Philosophy*, 3 (1998).

19 Aristotle, *Den nikomakiske etikk*, trans. Øyvind Rabbås and Anfinn Stigen (Oslo, 1999), p. 52 (1115a), and classics.mit.edu/Aristotle/nicomachaen.mb.txt.

20 Martin Heidegger, *Sein und Zeit* (Tübingen, 1986), p. 140.

21 Ernst Cassirer, *An Essay on Man: An Introduction to a Philosophy of Human Culture* (Garden City, NY, 1954), pp. 42–3.

22 Ernest Becker, *Escape from Evil* (New York, 1975), p. 148.

23 Thucydides, *Peloponneserkrigen, Første bind*, trans. Henning Mørland (Oslo, 1999), book 1.23 (§28); 1.88 (§61).

24 For such an examination, with the emphasis on fear and angst, see Isaac M. Marks and Randolph M. Nesse, 'Fear and Fitness: An Evolutionary Analysis of Anxiety Disorders', *Ethology and Sociobiology*, 15 (1994).

25 François de La Rochefoucauld, *Reflections; or, Sentences and Moral Maxims*, trans. J. W. Willis Bund and J. Hain Friswell (2007 edn), § 27.

26 Lucretius, *Om tingenes natur*, trans. Trygve Sparre (Oslo, 1978), p. 86, and classics.mit.edu/Carus/nature_things.3.iii.html.

27 William James, 'What is an Emotion?', *Mind*, 9 (1884), p. 190.

28 W. B. Cannon, 'The James-Lange Theory of Emotion: A Critical Examination and an Alternative Theory', *American Journal of Psychology*, 39 (1927). See also W. B. Cannon, *Bodily Changes in Pain, Fear and Rage* (New York, 1929).

29 Stanley Schachter and Jerome Singer, 'Cognitive, Social and Physiological Determinants of Emotional State', *Psychological Review*, 69 (1962).

30 Cf. Martha C. Nussbaum, *Upheavals of Thought: The Intelligence of the Emotions* (Cambridge, 2001), pp. 35–6.

31 For a good discussion of this, see Ronald de Sousa, 'Self-deceptive Emotions', in *Explaining Emotions*, ed. Amélie Oksenberg Rorty (Berkeley, CA, 1980), pp. 283–97.

32 'Furcht über einen unbestimmten Übel drohenden Gegenstand ist Bangigkeit.' Immanuel Kant, *Anthropologie in pragmatischer Hinsicht* (Berlin, 1968), §76, p. 255.

33 Precisely this point – to what extent I actually have to believe in the existence of fictional characters in order to feel fear in relation to them – is in fact a highly debated issue in non-fictional literature. I do not, however, intend to pursue this discussion here. For a quite easy-to-read presentation of the central issues, see Noël Carroll, *The Philosophy of Horror; or, Paradoxes of the Heart* (London and New York, 1990), chap. 2.

34 Elias Canetti, *Masse og makt*, trans. Niels Magnus Bugge (Oslo, 1995), p. 9.

35 H. P. Lovecraft, 'Supernatural Horror in Literature', in *At the Mountains of Madness* (New York, 2005), p. 105.

36 Aristotle, *Den nikomakiske etikk*, p. 54 (1115b).

37 Michel de Montaigne, 'Om frykten', in *Essays: Første bok*, trans. Beate Vibe (Oslo, 2004), p. 110.

38 Edmund Burke, *Philosophical Inquiry into the Origin of our Ideas of the Sublime and the Beautiful* (Oxford, 1998), p. 53.

39 Heidegger, *Sein und Zeit*, p. 342.

40 Cf. Damasio, *Følelsen av hva som skjer*, pp. 68–72.

41 Aristotle, *Retorikk*, trans. Tormod Eide (Oslo, 2006), p. 121 (1382a).

42 Thomas Hobbes, *De cive* (Oxford, 1983), book 1.2, pp. 58ff.

43 Adam Smith, *The Theory of Moral Sentiments* (Indianapolis, 1982), p. 30.

44 David Hume, *A Treatise of Human Nature* (London, 1984), book 2.9, p. 486.

45 Aristotle, *Retorikk*, p. 123 (1383a). It should be pointed out here that Aristotle is not completely consistent, since he also suggests: 'The coward is thus a person without hope, since he fears everything.' (Aristotele: *Den nikomakiske etikk*, p. 54, 1116a).

46 Thomas Aquinas, *Orden og mysterium*, trans. Vegard Skånland (Oslo, 1964), p. 90, no. 310.

47 Ibid., p. 90, no. 311.

48 For an easy-to-read and informative discussion of courage, see William Ian Miller, *The Mystery of Courage* (Cambridge, MA, and London, 2000).

49 Aristotle, *On Generation and Corruption*, in *The Complete Works of Aristotle*, (Princeton, NJ, 1985), 323b1ff. See also *Metafysikken*, in *The Complete Works of Aristotle*, 1002b15.

50 For a readable article that claims we are not at all passively at the mercy of our passions, and that they are not simply something one 'receives', see Robert C. Solomon, 'On the Passivity of the Passions', in *Not Passion's Slave: Emotions and Choice* (Oxford, 2003).

51 Heidegger, *Sein und Zeit*, p. 141.

52 Ibid., p. 137.

53 Martin Heidegger, *Nietzsche: Erster Band* (Pfullingen, 1989), p. 119.

54 Ibid., pp. 62–3.

55 Martin Heidegger, 'Was ist Metaphysik?', in *Wegmarken,
    Gesamtausgabe Bd*, IX (Frankfurt am Main, 1976), p. 111, and
    evans-experientialism.freewebspace.com/heidegger5a.htm.

56 Heidegger, *Sein und Zeit*, p. 140.

57 Ibid., p. 141.

58 Ibid., p. 342: 'Die Zeitlichkeit der Furcht ist ein gewärtigend-
    gegenwärtigendes Vergessen'.

59 Jean-Paul Sartre, *Erfaringer med de Andre*, trans. Dag
    Østerberg and Halvor Roll (Oslo, 1980), p. 146.

60 Jean-Paul Sartre, *The Emotions: Outline of a Theory*, trans. B.
    Frechtman (New York, 1986), p. 63.

61 Ibid., pp. 52ff.

62 Ibid., pp. 78–9, 84.

63 G.W.F. Hegel, *Enzyklopädie der philosophischen
    Wissenschaften I: Werke*, VIII (Frankfurt am Main, 1986),
    §410. See also Aristotle, *Den nikomakiske etikk*, 1152a, 25ff.

64 As Maurice Merleau-Ponty puts it, 'one says that the body
    has understood and the habit has been acquired when it has
    allowed itself to be permeated by a new meaning, when it
    has acquired a new core of meaning' (*Kroppens fenomenologi*,
    p. 103).

65 Cf. Isaac Marks, *Living with Fear: Understanding and Coping
    with Anxiety* (Maidenhead, 2005).

66 Cf. Brian Massumi, 'Everywhere You Want to Be:
    Introduction to Fear', in *The Politics of Everyday Fear*, ed.
    Brian Massumi (Minneapolis and London 1993), p. 24. See
    also Brian Massumi, 'Fear (The Spectrum Said)', *Positions*,
    XIII/1 (2005).

67 Zygmunt Bauman, *Liquid Fear* (Cambridge, 2006), p. 3.

THREE Fear and Risk

1 Anthony Giddens, *Modernity and Self-Identity: Self and
   Identity in the Late Modern Age* (Cambridge, 1991), p. 3.

2   Ulrich Beck, *Risk Society: Towards a New Modernity*
    (London, 1992), p. 96.
3   Don DeLillo, *White Noise* (New York, 1984), p. 35.
4   Ibid., p. 22.
5   Ibid., pp. 174–5.
6   Ibid., p. 114.
7   Ibid., p. 193.
8   See in particular Mary Douglas, *Risk and Blame: Essays in Cultural Theory* (London, 1992).
9   Those with a *realistic* view of risk believe that reality tran-
    scends our conceptions of it, and a risk is an objective fact.
    Social constructivists believe that a risk is basically a social
    entity, that it is shaped by the social environment of the
    players. Social constructivism does not consider knowledge
    of a risk as objectively related to an independent, external
    reality, but rather to the social groups that formulate them. I
    do not intend to take up this discussion here – and I myself
    adopt a moderate intermediate position. In doing so, I agree
    with, for example, Ulrich Beck, who sees strengths and weak-
    nesses in both positions, where the one position captures the
    objective and measurable aspects of risk but does not take
    into account that these are always situated in a cultural and
    political context, while the other position does the opposite.
    For a lucid description of this position, see Ulrich Beck,
    Ecological Politics in an Age of Risk (London, 1995).
10 With Aaron Wildavsky, Mary Douglas cites the Lele people,
    who are exposed to a number of diseases and dangerous
    natural phenomena, but who emphasize lightning strikes,
    infertility and bronchitis in their thinking about risk. Other
    groups and peoples emphasize other dangers. Mary Douglas
    and Aaron Wildavsky, *Risk and Culture: An Essay on the
    Selection of Technological and Environmental Dangers*
    (Berkeley, Los Angeles and London, 1982), p. 7.
11 Ibid.
12 Beck, *Risk Society*, p. 176.

13 Douglas, *Risk and Blame*, p. 26.

14 David L. Altheide, *Creating Fear: News and the Construction of Crisis* (New York, 2002), p. 147.

15 Cf. Frank Furedi, *Culture of Fear: Risk-taking and the Morality of Low Expectation*, revd edn (London and New York, 2005), p. 99.

16 Cf. Peter N. Stearns and Timothy Haggerty, 'The Role of Fear: Transitions in American Emotional Standards for Children, 1850–1950', *American Historical Review*, 96 (1991).

17 Cf. Joanna Bourke, *Fear: A Cultural History* (London, 2005), pp. 87ff.

18 Cf. Paul Slovic, *The Perception of Risk* (London, 2000), pp. 106–7.

19 Garric Blalock et al., 'The Impact of 9/11 on Driving Fatalities: The Other Lives Lost to Terrorism', www.news.cornell.edu/stories/March05/Sept11driving.pdf. We are often told of the dangers of driving a car, but an investigation concluded that the most dangerous of all means of transport was the oldest – walking (cf. Michelle Ernst, *Mean Streets 2004*, Surface Transportation Policy Project 2004). 'Safe' transport would thus seem to be an impossibility.

20 Slovic, *The Perception of Risk*, chap. 16.

21 Cf. Cass R. Sunstein, *Laws of Fear: Beyond the Precautionary Principle* (Cambridge, 2005), p. 82.

22 Slovic, *The Perception of Risk*, p. 323.

23 The objection can be raised here that those who die of ordinary influenza are, on the whole, old people with an already weakened state of health – and that these people, from a statistical point of view, would soon have died anyway. Viewed thus, the comparison can be slightly misleading.

24 For an informative and easy-to-read book that has this perspective, see Jan Brøgger sr., *Epidemier: En natur- og kulturhistorie* (Oslo, 2002).

25 info.cancerresearchuk.org/cancerstats/survival/latestrates/

26 www.pfizer.no/templates/NewsPage_1217.aspx

27 A. J. Wakefield et al., 'Ileal-Lymphoid-Nodular Hyperplasia, Non-Specific Colitis, and Pervasive Developmental Disorder in Children', in *The Lancet*, CCCLI/9103 (1998).

28 For a good, easy-to-read account of the whole Wakefield issue, see Michael Fitzpatrick, 'The MMR Story', in *Panic Nation*, ed. Stanley Feldman and Vincent Marks (London, 2005).

29 See Ståle Fredriksen, *Bad Luck and the Tragedy of Modern Medicine*, Medicine Faculty, University of Oslo (Oslo, 2005).

30 See Michel Foucault, *The Birth of the Clinic: An Archaeology of Medical Perception*, trans. A. M. Sheridan (London, 1997), especially chap. 9.

31 Zygmunt Bauman, *Flytende modernitet*, trans. Mette Nygård (Oslo, 2001), p. 95.

32 A classic discussion of this problem is Ivan Illich, *Medisinsk nemesis*, trans. Truls Hoff (Oslo, 1975).

33 John Krebs, 'Why Natural May Not Equal Healthy', in *Nature*, 415 (2002), p. 117.

34 Cf. Lakshman Karalliedde, 'Pesticides in Food', in *Panic Nation*.

35 For an easy-to-read account of the scientific studies within the field, which conclude that this research does not provide a basis for preferring organic farming to conventional farming, see Alex Avery, *The Truth About Organic Foods* (Chesterfield, MO, 2006).

36 Cf. Furedi, *Culture of Fear*, p. 57.

37 Ronald M. Davis and Barry Pless, '*BMJ* bans "accidents"', *British Medical Journal*, 322 (2001), pp. 1320–21.

38 Fredriksen, *Bad Luck and the Tragedy of Modern Medicine*.

39 See Christopher Frayling, *Mad, Bad and Dangerous? The Scientist and the Cinema* (London, 2005).

40 Beck, *Risk Society*, p. 183.

41 Niklas Luhmann, *Risk: A Sociological Theory*, trans. Rhodes Barrett (New York, 1993), p. 44.

42 Hans Jonas, *Das Prinzip Verantvortung: Versuch einer Ethik für die technologische Zivilisation* (Frankfurt am Main, 1979), p. 63.

43 Ibid., p. 391.

44 Harvey Scodel, 'An Interview with Professor Hans Jonas', *Social Research*, 2 (2003), p. 367.

45 The following discussion of the precautionary principle is greatly indebted to Sunstein, *Laws of Fear*.

46 Some theorists also link the precautionary principle to the so-called maximin principle, which says that alternatives ought to be ordered according to their worst conceivable result, and to eliminate the worst of the worst, so that one is left with the alternative that the worst case has a less bad result than the others. A problem about the maximin principle is that it does not take probability into account – only what the worst conceivable result is. Moreover, it can easily generate absurd consequences, e.g., that one ought not to try and combat global warming, because this would be very expensive without it necessarily being successful, and it is a worse result to use a lot of resources and yet still have the problem of global warming than it is to have global warming without using a lot of resources.

47 Sandy Starr, 'Science, Risk and the Price of Precaution', www.spiked-online.com/Articles/00000006DD7A.htm.

48 See C. Anderson, 'Cholera Epidemic Traced to Risk Miscalculation', *Nature*, 354 (1991), p. 255. Some people have claimed that the cholera outbreak cannot be traced so unequivocally to chlorine no longer being used in the water, since the possible causes are much more complex. See Joel Tickner and Tami Gouveia-Vigeant, 'The 1991 Cholera Epidemic in Peru: Not a Case of Precaution Gone Awry', *Risk Analysis*, 3 (2005), pp. 495ff.

49 The literature on DDT and malaria has become quite comprehensive. For a relatively easy-to-read yet thorough presentation and discussion, see Richard Tren and Roger Bate, 'Malaria and the DDT Story', *IEA Occasional Paper*, 117 (2001).

50 Frank Furedi, *Politics of Fear* (London and New York, 2005), p. 10.

51 Ibid., p. 11.

52 François Ewald, 'Two Infinities of Risk', in *The Politics of Everyday Fear*, ed. Brian Massumi (Minneapolis and London, 1993), pp. 221–2.

53 Ibid., pp. 227–8.

FOUR The Attraction of Fear

1 Friedrich Nietzsche, *Morgenröte, Kritische Studienausgabe*, III (Munich, Berlin and New York 1988), §551.

2 For a good overview of the history of the Gothic as a genre, see Richard Davenport, *Gothic: 400 Years of Excess, Horror, Evil and Ruin* (London, 1998).

3 Oscar Wilde, *Complete Works* (London, 1966), p. 1038.

4 Cf. Gerard Jones, *Drep monstrene: Barns behov for fantastiske forestillinger, superhelter og liksom-vold*, trans. Sigrid Salen (Oslo, 2004).

5 Jean Genet, *Tyvens dagbok*, trans. Herbert Svenkerud (Oslo, 1986), p. 7.

6 Ibid., p. 194.

7 Ibid., pp. 18–19.

8 Ibid., p. 179.

9 Quoted from Hagerup, 'Postscript', in Charles Baudelaire, *Spleen og Ideal*, trans. Haakon Dahlen (Oslo, 1999), p. 142.

10 Baudelaire, 'Hymne til venleiken', in *Spleen og Ideal*, pp. 41–2.

11 Baudelaire, 'Til lesaren', in *Spleen og Ideal*, p. 11.

12 Charles Baudelaire, *Dagbøker*, trans. Tore Stubberud (Oslo, 1975), p. 33.

13 This essay and a large number of De Quincey's texts on the same subject have been collected in Thomas De Quincey, *On Murder*, ed. Robert Morrison (Oxford, 2006). The following presentation of De Quincey is indebted to Joel Black, *The*

146

Aesthetics of Murder: A Study in Romantic Literature and Contemporary Culture (Baltimore and London, 1991).

14 De Quincey, *On Murder*, p. 11.

15 Edmund Burke, *Philosophical Inquiry into the Origin of our Ideas of the Sublime and the Beautiful* (Oxford, 1998), p. 43.

16 Ibid., p. 44.

17 Ibid., pp. 36, 79.

18 Ibid., p. 54.

19 Ibid., p. 42.

20 Rainer Maria Rilke, *Duineser Elegien* (Munich, 1997), and www.tonykline.co.uk/PITBR/German/Rilke.htm.

21 Immanuel Kant, *Beobachtungen über das Gefühl des Schönen und Erhabenen*, in *Kants gesammelte Schriften*, XI (Berlin and New York, 1902–) See also Immanuel Kant, *Bemerkungen zu den Beobachtungen über das Gefühl des Schönen und Erhabenen*, in *Kants gesammelte Schriften*, vol. XX.

22 Immanuel Kant, *Kritikk av dømmekraften*, trans. Espen Hammer (Oslo, 1995), §23, p. 118.

23 Ibid., §28, p. 136, and ebooks.adelaide.edu.au/k/kant/ immanuel /k16j/part8.html#ss28.

24 Burke, *Philosophical Inquiry*, p. 53.

25 Kant, *Kritikk av dømmekraften*, §28, p. 135.

26 Ibid., §29, p. 144–5.

27 Ibid., §28, p. 135.

28 Ibid., §28, pp. 137–8.

29 Quoted from Paul Oppenheimer, *Evil and the Demonic: A New Theory of Monstrous Behaviour* (New York, 1996), p. 79.

30 Kant, *Kritikk av dømmekraften*, §26, p. 127.

31 Don DeLillo, *White Noise* (New York, 1984), pp. 127–8.

32 Friedrich Nietzsche, *Nachgelassene Fragmente 1884–1885*, in *Kritische Studienausgabe*, vol. XI, (Munich, Berlin and New York, 1988), pp. 267–8.

33 Michel Foucault, *Det moderne fengsels historie*, trans. Dag Østerberg (Oslo, 1977), p. 64.

34 John Gay, *The Beggar's Opera* (London, 1987), Act I, scene 4, p. 12.

35 Friedrich von Schiller, 'Gedanken über den Gebrauch des Gemeinen und Niedrigen in der Kunst' [1802], in *Sämtliche Werke in fünf Bänden*, v (Munich, 2004).

36 In this connection it ought to be mentioned that Burke retracted his earlier statements on the Sublime more than 30 years later in *Reflections on the Revolution in France*, and that the older Burke would have denied that the terrorist attack was 'Sublime'. For a readable account of this, see Christine Battersby, 'Terror, Terrorism and the Sublime: Rethinking the Sublime after 1789 and 2001', *Postcolonial Studies*, 1 (2003), pp. 70–77.

37 De Quincey, *On Murder*, pp. 12–13.

38 Ibid., pp. 30-33.

39 Walter Benjamin, *Kunstverket i reproduksjonstidsalderen*, trans. Torodd Karlsten (Oslo, 1991).

40 Karl Rosenkranz, *Ästhetik des Hässlichen* (Leipzig, 1990).

41 Burke, *Philosophical Inquiry*, p. 109.

42 Aristotle, *Om diktekunsten*, trans. Sam Ledsaak (Oslo, 1989), p. 30, and www.gutenberg.org/dirs/etext99/poetc10.txt.

43 Ibid., pp. 35, 44, 48.

44 Aristotle, *Den nikomakiske etikk*, trans. Øyvind Rabbås and Anfinn Stigen (Oslo, 1999), p. 1104 b13.

45 De Quincey, *On Murder*, p. 32, and www.gutenberg.org/etext/10708.

46 For a readable discussion of this, see Noël Carroll, *The Philosophy of Horror; or, Paradoxes of the Heart* (London and New York, 1990), chap. 4.

47 Ibid., p. 7.

48 Cf. Maurice Merleau-Ponty, *Øyet og ånden*, trans. Mikkel B. Tin (Oslo, 2000).

49 For a good discussion of Burke on this point, see Richard Shusterman, 'Somaesthetics and Burke's Sublime', *British Journal of Aesthetics*, 4 (2005).

50 Chuck Palahniuk, *Fight Club* (New York, 1996), p. 155.
51 Ibid., p. 148.
52 John Locke, *An Essay Concerning Human Understanding* (Oxford, 1975), Book II, chap. 21.
53 Jean Delumeau, *Sin and Fear: The Emergence of Western Guilt Culture, 13th–18th Centuries*, trans. Eric Nicholson (New York, 1990), p. 555.

FIVE Fear and Trust

1 Knud Ejler Løgstrup, *Den etiske fordring* (Copenhagen, 1956), pp. 17–18.
2 BBC news, 'Britain is "Surveillance Society"', 2 November 2006: news.bbc.co.uk/1/hi/uk/6108496.stm.
3 Ulrich Beck, *Weltrisikogesellschaft: Auf der Suche nach der Verlorenen Sicherheit* (Frankfurt am Main, 2007), p. 335.
4 Gavin de Becker, *The Gift of Fear: Survival Signals that Protect Us from Violence* (New York, 1997).
5 Ibid., p. 66.
6 Ibid., p. 80.
7 For a sociological analysis of this perspective of dependency, see Anthony Giddens, *The Transformations of Intimacy* (Oxford, 1992), chap. 6.
8 Francis Fukuyama, *Trust: The Social Virtues and the Creation of Prosperity* (New York, 1996).
9 Cf. Niklas Luhmann, *Vertrauen: Ein Mechanismus der Reduktion sozialer Komplxität* (Stuttgart, 2000).
10 Fukuyama, *Trust*, pp. 27, 152–8.
11 Løgstrup, *Den etiske fordring*, p. 28.
12 Ernst Fehr and Bettina Rockenbach, 'Detrimental Effects of Sanctions on Human Altruism', *Nature*, 422 (2003), pp. 137–40.
13 Andreas Olsson et al., 'The Role of Social Groups in the Persistence of Learned Fear', *Science*, 309 (2005).

14 Arne Öhman, 'Conditioned Fear of a Face: A Prelude to
    Ethnic Enmity?', *Science*, 309 (2005).
15 Robert C. Solomon and Fernando Flores, *Building Trust in
    Business, Politics, Relationships and Life* (Oxford and New
    York, 2001), p. 22.
16 Georg Simmel, *Philosophie des Geldes, Gesamtausgabe*, VI
    (Frankfurt am Main, 1989), p. 215.
17 Georg Simmel, *Soziologie: Untersuchungen über die Formen
    der Vergesellschaftung* II (Frankfurt am Main, 1989), p. 393.
18 Ibid.
19 Simmel, *Philosophie des Geldes*, p. 215.
20 Translated from Dietrich Bonhoeffer, *Motstand og hengivelse:
    Brev og opptegnelser fra fengselet*, trans. Svein Hanssen-Bauer
    (Oslo, 2000), p. 36.
21 The following distinction between naive trust, stupid trust
    and reflected trust coincides to a great extent with that
    between 'simple trust', 'blind trust' and 'authentic trust' in
    Solomon and Flores, *Building Trust in Business, Politics,
    Relationships, and Life*, pp. 37–8, 64–5, 91–103.
22 Paul Slovic, *The Perception of Risk* (London, 2000), chap. 19.

six The Politics of Fear

1 For a study that takes this perspective a long way, see Elemér
   Hankiss, *Fears and Symbols: An Introduction to the Study of
   Western Civilisation* (Budapest, 2001).
2 Giambattista Vico, *The New Science* (Ithaca, NY, 1984),
   §§379–91.
3 Thomas Hobbes, *De Cive* (Oxford, 1983), chap. 2.
4 Niccolò Machiavelli, *Discorsi: En drøftelse av Titus Livius' ti
   første bøker*, 3 vols, trans. Jon Bingen (Oslo, 2004), vol. I,
   book 1.3, p. 24, and www.gutenberg.org/ebooks/15772.
5 I discuss the extent to which man is basically good, evil or
   both in Lars F. H. Svendsen, *Ondskapens filosofi* (Oslo, 2001),

pp. 74–8.

6 Niccolò Machiavelli, *Fyrsten*, trans. Jon Bingen (Oslo, 1988), chap. 8.7, p. 49.

7 Ibid., chap. 8.8., p. 49.

8 Ibid., chap. 17.1, p. 88.

9 Ibid., chap. 18.4, p. 93, and chap. 9.5, p. 53.

10 Ibid., chap. 17.1, p. 87.

11 Ibid., chap. 17.2, p. 89.

12 Thomas Hobbes, *Leviathan* (Cambridge, 1991), chap. 14, p. 99.

13 Hobbes, *De Cive*, pp. 58–9. Cf. Thomas Hobbes, *Leviathan*, chap. 13, p. 89.

14 Hobbes, *Leviathan*, chap. 13.

15 Ibid., chap. 13, pp. 88–9.

16 Ibid., chap. 13, pp. 89.

17 Ibid., chap. 27, p. 206.

18 Ibid., chap. 13, p. 90.

19 Immanuel Kant, *Grundlegung zur Metaphysik der Sitten, i Kants gesammelte Schriften*, VIII (Berlin and New York, 1902–), p. 401n. For Kant's overall criticism of Hobbes's political philosophy, see Immanuel Kant, *Über den Gemeinspruch: Das mag in der Theorie richtig sein, taugt aber nicht für die Praxis*, in *Kants gesammelte Schriften*, VIII (Berlin and New York 1902–), part 2, pp. 289–306.

20 Hobbes, *Leviathan*, chap. 21, p. 146.

21 See ibid., chap. 30.

22 Cf. Gregory S. Kavka: 'Rule by Fear', *Nous*, 4 (1983).

23 See Alexis de Tocqueville, *Democracy in America*, trans. and ed. H. C. Mansfield and D. Winthrop (Chicago, 2000); *Om demokratiet i Amerika*, trans. Birgit Tønnesson (Oslo, 1995).

24 Michael Ignatieff, *The Warrior's Honor: Ethnic War and the Modern Conscience* (New York, 1997), p. 18.

25 Judith N. Shklar, *Political Thought and Political Thinkers* (Chicago, 1998), chap. 1.

26 Cf. Tom Pyszcynski, 'What Are We So Afraid Of? A Terror Management Perspective on the Politics of Fear', *Social Research*, 4 (2004), pp. 837–8.

27 Ralph Waldo Emerson, 'Self-Reliance', in *The Essential Writings of Ralph Waldo Emerson* (New York, 2000).

28 I have discussed this in more detail in Lars F. H. Svendsen: 'Ondskapens retorikk', *Morgenbladet*, 13 September 2002.

29 Jf. François Debrix, 'Tabloid Realism and the Revival of American Security Culture', *Geopolitics*, 3 (2003).

30 Samuel Huntington, *The Clash of Civilisations and the Remaking of World Order* (New York, 1996), p. 302.

31 Zbigniew Brzezinski, *Out of Control: Global Turmoil on the Eve of the Twenty-First Century* (New York, 1993), and *The Grand Chessboard: American Primacy and Its Geostratic Imperatives* (New York, 1997), Robert D. Kaplan, *The Coming Anarchy: Shattering the Dreams of the Post-Cold War* (New York, 2000).

32 See, for example, John Mueller, *Overblown: How Politicians and the Terrorism Industry Inflate National Security Threats, and Why We Believe Them* (New York, 2006).

33 See Department of Homeland Security, *Progress in Developing the National Asset Database*, Washington, DC, June 2006.

34 www.usdoj.gov/oig/reports/plus/a0720/final.pdf.

35 Machiavelli, *Fyrsten*, chap. 9.7, p. 55, and www.gutenberg.org/etext/1232.

36 Robb Willer, 'The Effects of Government-Issued Terror Warnings on Presidential Approval Ratings', *Current Research in Social Psychology*, 10 (2004).

37 George W. Bush, 'Presidentens tale om rikets tilstand', *Morgenbladet – bilag om Irak-krisen*, 14 March 2003, pp. 26–8, and www.whitehouse.gov/news/releases/2003/01/20030128-19.html.

38 Cf. Eric Alterman, 'Fear: What Is It Good For?', *Social Research*, 4 (2004), p. 1008.

39 Cf. Max Rodenbeck, 'How Terrible Is It?', *New York Review of Books*, 19 (2006).

40 www.angus-reid.com/polls/index.cfm/fuseaction/viewItem/ itemID/14948.

41 I have also discussed this in the epilogue to the 2nd edition of my book *Ondskapens filosofi* (2002).

42 Mark Mazzetti: 'Spy Agencies Say Iraq War Worsens Terror Threat', *New York Times*, 24 September 2006.

43 *National Strategy for Combating Terrorism* (2003), p. 1.

44 Ibid., p. 1 and p. 30.

45 Ibid., p. 1.

46 www.whitehouse.gov/news/releases/2002/06/20020601-3.html.

47 Michael Ignatieff, *The Lesser Evil: Political Ethics in an Age of Terror* (Princeton, NJ, 2004).

48 Cf. Yaseen Noorani, 'The Rhetoric of Security', CR: *The New Centennial Review*, 1 (2005).

49 Ulrich Beck, 'The Silence of Words: On Terror and War', *Security Dialogue*, 3 (2003), p. 263.

50 Carl Schmitt, *Der Begriff des Politischen* [1932] (Berlin, 1996), p. 37.

51 The most radical proposal was formulated in *The Domestic Security Enhancement Act* (www.publicintegrity.org/docs/ PatriotAct/story_01_020703_doc_1.pdf). The document contained a clause that every American citizen supporting an activity by an organization that the American authorities judge to be terrorist can lose his or her citizenship. In short, this meant that a citizen can be deported if that person's presence in the US can be defined as contravening national interests. This bill from the American Justice Department, which was leaked in February 2003, was never put forward as an official proposal, but it is worth noting that it was taken to the level of an official draft. Such a radical proposal would, even so, have had little possibility of being approved, but it fits in as a continuance of other encroachments on the freedom of the individual.

52 www.cnn.com/2005/POLITICS/12/19/nsa/index.html

53 The Bush administration, for example, has done much to undermine the principle of the separation of powers and to give the executive authority (the president) far greater authority than is warranted by the separation of powers. See Elizabeth Drew, 'Power Grab', *New York Review of Books*, 11 (2006).

54 Quoted from Louise Richardson, *What Terrorists Want* (New York, 2006), p. 205, and www.brainyquote.com/quotes/quotes/b/benjaminfr110256.html.

55 Ibid., pp. 5ff.

56 For an easy-to-read, well-informed study of the concept of 'terrorist' – and the problems involved in arriving at a definition of it – see Phil Rees, *Dining with Terrorists*, 2nd edn (London, 2005).

57 See Svendsen, *Ondskapens filosofi*.

58 I have made some tentative attempts at this in *Ondskapens filosofi*, pp. 195–210. For a readable discussion of the problem, see, for example, John Keane, *Reflections on Violence* (London and New York, 1996).

59 Cf. Chris Sparks, 'Liberalism, Terrorism and the Politics of Fear', *Politics*, 3 (2003).

60 Richardson, *What Terrorists Want*, p. 142.

61 Michael Walzer, 'On Negative Politics', in *Liberalism without Illusions*, ed. Bernard Yack (Chicago, IL, 1996).

SEVEN Beyond Fear?

1 Adam Phillips, *Terrors and Experts* (Cambridge, MA, 1997), p. 46.

2 Cf. Eric A. Posner and Adrian Vermule, 'Accomodating Emergencies', *Stanford Law Review*, 56 (2003).

3 Giorgio Agamben, 'The State of Emergency', www.generation-online.org/p/fpagambenschmitt.htm.

4 Wole Soyinka, *Climate of Fear* (London, 2004), p. 46.

5 news.bbc.co.uk/1/hi/world/americas/4292114.stm

6 Cf. Frank Furedi, *Culture of Fear: Risk-taking and the Morality of Low Expectation*, revd edn (London and New York, 2005), p. 53.

7 Soyinka, *Climate of Fear*, p. 5.

8 Michel de Montaigne, 'Om erfaring', in *Essays*, trans. Beate Vibe (Oslo, 1996), p. 287.

9 Joseph Conrad, 'An Outpost of Progress', in *'Heart of Darkness' and Other Tales* (Oxford, 1990), p. 21.

10 Aldous Huxley, *Vidunderlige nye verden* (Oslo, 1982), p. 181.

11 J. G. Ballard, *Running Wild* (London, 1988).

12 During the 1990s, reports also appeared of over-protective parents giving their children 'adventure deficit disorder', that is, the children lacked excitement in their lives (Cf. Renata Salecl, *On Anxiety*, London, 2004, p. 3.) To talk about this as a mental disorder is first and foremost part of the general inflation within this area, but at the same time it indicates that we don't feel well when our lives are too protected.

13 Chuck Palahniuk, *Invisible Monsters* (London, 1999), p. 256.

14 For perspectives on pessimism as a mode of thought, see, for example, Joe Bailey, *Pessimism* (London and New York, 1988); Oliver Bennett, *Cultural Pessimism: Narratives of Decline in the Postmodern World* (Edinburgh, 2001); Michael Pauen, *Pessimismus: Geschichtsphilosophie, Metaphysik und Moderne von Nietzsche bis Spengler* (Berlin, 1997)

15 For readable studies of the logic and history of the idea of progress, see Friedrich Rapp, *Fortschritt: Entwicklung und Sinngehalt einer philosophischen Idee* (Darmstadt, 1992); Robert Nisbet, *History of the Idea of Progress* (New York, 1980).

16 Zygmunt Bauman, *Flytende Modernitet*, trans. Mette Nygård (Oslo, 2001), p. 153.

17 Ernst Bloch, *Das Prinzip Hoffnung*, vol. I (Frankfurt am Main, 1985), p. 1.

18 Francis Herbert Bradley, *Aphorisms* (Oxford, 1930), §63.